The Christian Poet

in

Paradise Lost

. . . my advent'rous Song . . .

WILLIAM G. RIGGS

The Christian Poet
in
Paradise Lost

University of California Press
Berkeley   Los Angeles   London
1972

University of California Press
Berkeley and Los Angeles, California
University of California Press, Ltd.
London, England
Copyright © 1972, by
The Regents of the University of California
ISBN: 0-520-02081-2
Library of Congress Catalog Card Number: 72-165237
Designed by Theo Jung
Printed in the United States of America

For Jan

Acknowledgments

I HAVE TRIED to document my most direct uses of Milton scholarship as they occur, but the extent of what has been written about Milton, combined with the deficiencies of my own memory, will undoubtedly make these specific acknowledgments seem somewhat whimsical to different readers who will recognize different debts unpaid. Here I can only record in a general way my obvious indebtedness to the continuing discussion of Milton's works and hope this book adds something to it.

Milton's poetry first became important to me in courses given by Hugh Richmond and Wayne Shumaker at the University of California at Berkeley. Ideas for this book began to take shape under Professor Richmond's guidance, and my greatest debt for advice and timely encouragement is to him. Norman Rabkin's sympathetic criticism was similarly a great help in the early stages of this work. More recently, Michael G. Cooke and Keith Stavely have assisted me with their suggestions and their kind interest; and both J. Martin Evans and Earl Miner have provided firm criticism which has preserved me from a number of confusions and errors. My thanks goes also to William J. McClung and Sheila Levine for editorial aid and council. Remaining inaccuracies are, of course, my own.

Boston University provided research funds and a summer grant which allowed me to complete this project. Chapter I has appeared in a slightly different form in *Milton Studies*, 2 (1970), edited by James D. Simmonds, and appears by permission of the University of Pittsburgh Press.

This book is dedicated to my wife whose tireless editing of my several manuscript versions has been the least of her labors.

Contents

Abbreviations

Introduction

I

AN ASPECT of *Paradise Lost* that most readers respond to is Milton's presence in the poem, a presence felt not only in the epic invocations and the other direct intrusions of the poet's voice but also in the shape and texture of the narrative itself. I wish here to examine this presence and to argue that the epic characters of Milton's poem are drawn with continued reference to the poet as he is portrayed in the four lyrical prologues. Milton's encounters with his own Satan, with Adam and Eve, the angels, and the Son were, I believe, a personal adventure in which he explored by deliberate comparison of himself to his characters what it means to be a Christian poet. My approach to Milton's poem seeks to locate the poet's vantage point, and I find, in pursuing the Christian poet in *Paradise Lost*, that Milton has presented himself to his reader as the prime example of the relevance of his biblical epic to fallen men.

In this self-directedness Milton's poem displays its affinities with other works of Baroque art[1] and, more nar-

[1] See Frederick Hartt's excellent study, *Love in Baroque Art* (Locust Valley, New York: J. J. Augustin for The Institute of Fine Arts, New York Univ., 1964).

rowly, with Puritan attitudes. With these Puritan affinities we may usefully begin. However uncongenial Puritan
belief may now seem to our sense of free expression, it
was the religious attitude fostered in large measure by
Puritanism—the developing insistence on the sanctity
of the individual conscience—which helped lay the foundations of a modern subjectivity, the subjectivity we find
taking shape in *Paradise Lost*. Milton himself did not
hesitate to endorse the Puritan confidence in the potential
of each man, Bible in hand and God in heart, to come to
his own terms with the universe. In *A Tretise of Civil
Power*, to pick one of many instances, Milton could
insist that

. . . no man or body of men in these times can be the infallible
judge or determiners in matters of religion to any other men's
consciences but their own. . . . God himself in many places
commands us by the same apostle [Paul], to search, to try, to
judge of these things ourselves: and gives us reason also, Ga.
vi, 4, 5: "Let every man prove his own work, and then shall he
have rejoicing in himself alone and not in another: for every
man shall bear his own burden."[2]

Milton displays here the characteristically Puritan emphasis on independence which created a conviction, in
the minds of the brethren, that every individual life was
a significant chronicle of God's dealings with man and
man's dealings with God—a conviction that produced
the flood of Puritan autobiography William Haller has
chronicled.[3] No less than subsequent apostles of private

[2] *The Works of John Milton*, Frank Allen Patterson, ed. (New
York: Columbia Univ. Press, 1931–1942), VI, 6. All citations of
Milton's prose works refer to this Columbia edition, hereafter
abbreviated C.E.

[3] William Haller, *The Rise of Puritanism* (New York: Columbia
Univ. Press, 1938).

experience, the Puritan was interested in himself, and Milton, to the disgust of some of his critics, shared this preoccupation. In his prose tracts, for example, the argument is repeatedly Milton the man;[4] and while the personal, *ad hominem* character of Milton's engagement in controversy was no innovation of seventeenth-century polemics,[5] the Puritan inclination to autobiography, as James Holly Hanford has told us, was also clearly at work:

> The personal passages were designed to exhibit the works of God in John Milton—to proclaim the fruits of faith, "his own faith not another's," in order that believers everywhere might be strengthened. The writing of this sort of spiritual autobiography, widely practiced among the Puritans, was the obligation of every man who felt conviction within himself, though ordinarily the record is less complicated by the secular and humanistic factors which are so strong in Milton.[6]

This estimate of Milton's autobiographical inclination refers primarily to the prose writings, but as most readers would attest Milton's concern with himself was by no means restricted to the works of his left hand. One may choose to prefer a poetless poem, but with Milton such a choice is inevitably strained, for in nearly all of Milton's poems the pressure of autobiography is a shaping factor. At times the poet Milton is a dramatic presence in his poems, and to insist that such presences be viewed without reference to Milton's life and personality is both

[4] See Milton's justification of this practice in *An Apology against a Pamphlet*, C.E., III, i, 284.

[5] John Diekhoff, "The Function of the Prologues in *Paradise Lost*," *PMLA*, 57 (1942), 697–704.

[6] James Holly Hanford, *A Milton Handbook* (New York: F. S. Crofts, 1938), p. 4.

artificial and distorting. Surely Milton has given us permission to look for him in his poetry; in *The Reason of Church Government* he goes as far as to suggest that poetry more than prose is the suitable vehicle for autobiography:

> For although a poet, soaring in the high region of his fancies with his garland and singing robes about him, might without apology speak more of himself than I mean to do, yet for me sitting here below in the cool element of prose, a mortal thing among many readers of no empyreal conceit to venture and divulge unusual things of myself, I shall petition to the gentler sort, it may not be envy to me.
>
> (C.E., III, i, 235)

The reason Milton finds poetry the proper place to "speak more of himself" is that he conceives of a unity between the speaker and his speech which is crucial. If poetry is the higher art, the need for a correspondingly more adequate account of the artist is necessary. In *An Apology Against a Pamphlet*, Milton explains why the poet must be accountable to his poem:

> And long it was not after, when I was confirm'd in this opinion, that he who would not be frustrate of his hope to write well hereafter in laudable things, ought him selfe to bee a true poem, that is, a composition, and patterne of the best and honourablest things; not presuming to sing high praises of heroick men, or famous Cities, unless he have in himselfe the experience and the practice of all that which is praise-worthy.
>
> (C.E., III, i, 303–304)

This ancient idea has had few more diligent subscribers than John Milton.

Since in Milton's mind the poet, himself a heroic pattern, may, "soaring in the high region of his fancies . . .

speak . . . of himself," it is not surprising that the figure
of the narrator should appear so prominently in *Paradise
Lost*. Four times in the course of his epic Milton pauses
to present himself to his readers. He appears "with his
garland and singing robes about him," but he is also
recognizably John Milton, blind and embattled in England's declining age. On each of these occasions his concern is with the relation between the poet as human singer
and the superhuman subject of his song. This relation
is a formative matter in *Paradise Lost*: it controls Milton's
sense of poetic decorum. Milton's cautious consideration
of his own strengths and weaknesses as inspired poet is
expressed not just in the poem's four prologues but
throughout his narrative—the argument of *Paradise
Lost* and its aesthetic principles are inseparable.[7]

Narrative poetry is full of poet-heroes (medieval narrative poetry is an obvious case in point), but in any common conception of an epic poem, the singer is not the
subject of his song. We do not, for example, call *The
Prelude* an epic without willfully distorting our conventional ideas of genre. Yet it is not just Wordsworth's
kind of poem in which the personality of the poet looms
large. Milton wrote in *The First Defense* that "Poets generally put something like their own opinions into the
mouths of their best characters" (C.E., VII, 327), and if
he thought that future ages would judge him personally
for opinions expressed through his characters, he was
certainly right. Both God and Satan have been virtually
identified with Milton, and while such impressionistic
identifications are facile, they also respond to the pres-

[7] For a similar comment see Dennis Burden, *The Logical Epic*
(Cambridge, Mass.: Harvard Univ. Press, 1967), p. 60.

ence of Milton as it is constantly felt in his epic poem.[8] Milton is no Joycean artist, removed from his subject, paring his nails. Rather he is closer to another pattern of the artist offered by Joyce's Stephen Dedalus, a critic whose definition of epic has, to my knowledge, been ignored by students of Milton. This definition, shorn of its historical apparatus, can tell us something about *Paradise Lost*:

The simplest epical form is seen emerging out of lyrical literature when the artist prolongs and broods upon himself as the centre of an epical event and this form progresses till the centre of emotional gravity is equidistant from the artist himself and from others. The narrative is no longer purely personal. The personality of the artist passes into the narration itself, flowing round and round the persons and actions like a vital sea.[9]

It would, perhaps, be superficial to point out that *Paradise Lost*, like Stephen's example, *Turpin Hero*, "begins in the first person and ends in the third."[10] But the picture of the artist, brooding "upon himself as the centre of an epical event," his personality passing "into the narration

[8] On Milton's presence in *Paradise Lost* see Dame Helen Gardner's concise and penetrating book, *A Reading of "Paradise Lost"* (Oxford: The Clarendon Press, 1967), p. 35:

> ... the universe of *Paradise Lost* is wholly undramatic, because the dramatist himself defies the first rule of dramatic presentation by being himself present throughout, as actor in his own play. He is not merely present in the beautiful prologues in which, going beyond all epic precedent, Milton takes the reader into the sanctuary of his own hopes and fears and sorrows, but he is present, as producer or presenter of his own drama, on the stage throughout.

[9] James Joyce, *A Portrait of the Artist as a Young Man* (New York: Viking Press, 1964), pp. 214–215.

[10] Joyce, p. 214.

itself, flowing round and round the persons and the actions like a vital sea," describes *Paradise lost* with remarkable aptness. In this study I will be applying Stephen's definition of "The simplest epical form" to Milton's poem by exploring the ways in which the epic's "persons and actions" inevitably and deliberately reflect the poet's own sense of himself.[11]

II

That the description of the poet in *Paradise Lost* contributes significantly to the epic's total design is not, of course, a new observation; it has, in fact, become commonplace in recent commentary on Milton's poetry. Few modern readers would agree with Dr. Johnson that Milton's self-descriptive prologues amount to "beautiful" "superfluities";[12] while we may not, today, wholly embrace Denis Saurat's rebuttal of Johnson in which the prologues become central to the epic and "The hero of

[11] Such a use of the poet in heroic poetry has its own tradition and has been explored by Robert Durling in *The Figure of the Poet in Renaissance Epic* (Cambridge, Mass.: Harvard Univ. Press, 1965). Durling, tracing the figure of the narrator in epic tradition from Virgil through the Renaissance to Spenser, frequently observes that the epic singer, as described in his poem, sees himself as involved in situations which parallel the situations of his principal characters (see in particular pp. 8, 160, 196). Given his topic, it seems odd that Durling should end his study with Spenser. Milton, the next obvious step in the course Durling follows, employs the figure of the narrator in a manner much more striking than any of his Renaissance predecessors. In fact, while the figure of the narrator remains distinctly tangential in the poems Durling treats, in *Paradise Lost* the particular concerns of the poet can lead us directly to the poem's thematic center.

[12] Samuel Johnson, *Works* (London, 1806), IX, 145.

Paradise Lost" becomes "Milton himself,"[13] our sense
that Milton's poem is unified in complex ways has produced a tempered version of Saurat's claim in which the
poet has become, through the poem's allusive texture, a
participant in his own narrative.[14] For the best of Milton's

[13] Denis Saurat, *Milton, Man and Thinker* (New York: Dial
Press, 1925), pp. 220, 213.

[14] Significant attempts to integrate the prologues with the rest of
Paradise Lost begin with E. M. W. Tillyard (*Milton* [London: Dial
Press, 1930]) who views their function as in the main transitional.
More recently Isabel MacCaffrey (*"Paradise Lost"* as *"Myth"*
[Cambridge, Mass.: Harvard Univ. Press, 1959]) sees the prologues
as "a series of passages in which Milton is to trace his own progress
through the poem" (p. 56), and she is followed in this opinion by
Louis L. Martz in *The Paradise Within* (New Haven: Yale Univ.
Press, 1964): "These personal touches are no mere self-indulgence;
they have a function—to remind us, intimately, that this poem is
an action of thoughts within a central, controlling intelligence
that moves with inward eyes toward a recovery of Paradise" (p.
106). The most detailed and illuminating study of the poet in *Paradise Lost* is Anne Davidson Ferry's book, *Milton's Epic Voice* (Cambridge, Mass.: Harvard Univ. Press, 1963). Mrs. Ferry looks squarely at the poetic texture of the prologues and demonstrates how
Milton's description of the poet as "bird and blind bard" is or-
ganically merged with "the total pattern of the poem—the cycle
of loss and restoration announced in the opening sentence and
expressed in the mood of its final lines" (p. 28). Like Mrs. Ferry,
Jackson I. Cope (*The Metaphoric Structure of "Paradise Lost"*
[Baltimore: Johns Hopkins Press, 1962]) observes that in *Paradise
Lost* the condition of blindness operates metaphorically to link
the poet with his poem (see especially pp. 85, 120, 164). Cope alters
Saurat's impressionistic "The hero of *Paradise Lost* is Milton
himself" to read "[Milton] finds himself a microcosmic mirror of
his own argument" (p. 120). How Milton finds himself such a
mirror will be my subject here—a subject in pursuit of which I
will frequently be incorporating and redeploying the work of these
critics. I am also pleased to note that Michael Lieb's book, *The
Dialectics of Creation* (Amherst: Univ. of Massachusetts Press,
1970), which was available to me only after my manuscript was

recent critics, analogical complexity is the principle of design in *Paradise Lost*. The epic's narrative, it is emphasized, repeatedly echoes itself, and the echoes serve to transform the chronologically transient occurrences of ordinary narrative into eternal paradigms.[15] Milton, in this view, consistently unifies his narrative materials (and his ontology) by explicit comparisons among the divine, the human, and the infernal. While Adam's disobedience seems in part the result of Satan's fall, it is also an echo of Satan's sin. The Son's missions of creation are played against the backdrop of Satan's circumstantially similar voyages of destruction. The first council in Heaven pointedly recalls the consult in Pandaemonium. Heavenly paternity is parodied by Satan and his hellish offspring. To modern critics, the range of such analogies has appeared vastly extendible and has recently been seen to circumscribe the reader as well as the poet.[16] Milton's rhetoric may well be intended to draw the reader into an analogical participation in the story of the fall, but it seems to me that such participation, if it is to begin, begins

complete, confirms in several ways the view of the poet I present here. See in particular Lieb's first chapter which, while differing from my presentation in many points of emphasis and detail, takes up the central issues discussed in Chapter IV of this book.

[15] In addition to works already cited by Tillyard, MacCaffrey, Cope, Ferry, and Martz, see in particular B. Rajan, *"Paradise Lost" and the Seventeenth Century Reader* (London: Chatto and Windus, 1947); Arnold Stein, *Answerable Style: Essays on "Paradise Lost"* (Minneapolis: Univ. of Minnesota Press, 1953). Joseph H. Summers, *The Muse's Method* (Cambridge, Mass.: Harvard Univ. Press, 1962); Stanley E. Fish, *Surprised by Sin* (New York: St. Martin's Press, 1967).

[16] See Fish and also Jon S. Lawry, *The Shadow of Heaven* (Ithaca, N.Y.: Cornell Univ. Press, 1968).

at second hand with a view of the poet, a character clearly placed within the analogical framework of *Paradise Lost* as an extended example of the relevance of Milton's cosmic drama to fallen man. To define his own position as Christian poet, Milton creates in the narrator of *Paradise Lost* a figure whose personal concerns are inextricably entwined with the concerns of his other epic characters— a figure who speaks to us of the difficulties and necessities of Christian action.[17]

Milton begins by telling us that the composition of *Paradise Lost* depends upon divine inspiration. This is, of course, conventional, but there is nothing conventional about the intensity with which Milton expresses his debt to God. Clearly the issue of divine inspiration is important to Milton, and one of the objectives of this study will be to define with care his attitude toward the muse. There is no question that Milton believed God could speak through inferior vessels of His choosing; that Milton hoped to be so chosen is also clear from the in-

[17] In her book Mrs. Ferry continually emphasizes the fictional aspect of the narrator in *Paradise Lost*, and by holding tight reins on this conception she is able to comment tellingly on Milton's style (see especially chapters II, III, and IV). Occasionally, however, I think it is useful to look beyond the conception of narrator as fictional character, at least far enough to be continually aware of how the intellectual matrix of the narrator as Milton controls the tone and direction of the poem. I am not suggesting a return to the biographical extravagances of Saurat. Everything I have to say will be measured against the text of *Paradise Lost*. But I think there is no need to handicap oneself by pretending that this text does not often bear the stamp of Milton's personal experience or that Milton's other writings cannot help us in the interpretive problems his great epic poses. It is not just metaphorical felicity or Christian tradition that makes the epic voice of *Paradise Lost* a blind man in search of light.

vocations of *Paradise Lost* which place Milton squarely in the prophetic line in their initial comparison of the poet to Moses. In these invocations Milton expresses a trust in God and a dependence on His aid for support in the composition of his masterwork. Yet a question clouds Milton's call for divine assistance: does a trust in God justify an absolute conviction in the matter of heavenly inspiration? Is not such an absolute conviction tantamount to spiritual pride? This is a delicate and ambiguous spiritual issue. "Oft-times," Raphael assures Adam, "nothing profits more / Than self-esteem grounded on just and right" (VIII, 571–572),[18] but in thinking of Milton, the man, the suspicion of overweening pride has proved hard to avoid. In particular the predominant impression one receives from Milton's early discussions of his own destiny is that his confidence not that God *can* but that God *will* choose him, by right of merit, amounts to unqualified certainty. In the famous autobiographical section of *The Reason of Church Government*, for example, Milton seems almost to preen himself before the mirror of what he hopes to accomplish:

Neither do I think it shame to covenant with any knowing reader, that for some few years yet I may go on trust with him toward the payment of what I am now indebted, as being a work not to be raised from the heat of youth, or the vapors of wine, like that which flows at waste from the pen of some vulgar amorist, or the trencher fury of a riming parasite, not to be obtained by the invocation of Dame Memory and her Siren Daughters, but by devout prayer to that eternal Spirit

[18] All citations of Milton's poems refer to *John Milton: Complete Poems and Major Prose*, ed. Merritt Y. Hughes (New York: Odyssey Press, 1957).

who can enrich with all utterance and knowledge, and purify
the lips of whom he pleases.

(C.E., III, i, 240–241)

While Milton leaves room here for God's pleasure, the
tone of this passage is palpably cocksure. Later, in
the midst of his accomplishment, he seems more sub-
dued, as when the chorus of *Samson Agonistes* feels, as
Milton must have felt, the apparent variability of God's
ways towards those "With gifts and graces eminently
adorn'd / To some great work" (679–680) or when Christ
on the pinnacle, having refused to presume on God's
benevolences, ends his agon still standing and waiting.
Milton, to be sure, never lost faith that God could "enrich with all utterance," but in his later years he appears
more sensitive to Christ's injunction, "Tempt not the
Lord thy God" (*Paradise Regained*, IV, 561). I will be
arguing here that this sensitivity to the dangers of spiritual presumption creates in *Paradise Lost* a tension in
Milton's attitude toward his inspiration, a tension which
affects significantly the epic's shape. Frequently, in dis-
cussing the relation of Milton's prologues to his poem,
I will return to one central contention: Milton's approach
to the writing of a work as monumental as *Paradise Lost*
was necessarily tentative; inspiration from God was crucial to his undertaking, but such inspiration could not be
commanded; it could only be hoped for, sought by prayer;
the choice of answering remained always with God, Milton's ultimate support and his final critic.

III

Like any long-established masterpiece, *Paradise Lost* has
been seen by many eyes, comprehended in many ways.

Like other masterworks its greatness resides partly in its
ability to maintain its power of impression—even as a
source of annoyance—from many angles of vision. Three
hundred years after Milton's death his major poem
offers few questions which have not already been asked;
it contains few central mysteries which have not yielded
variously to the ingenuity of twelve generations. *Paradise Lost*, in its broad outlines at least, is known, and
because of this perhaps the most the critic of today can
hope for in dealing with the poem whole is to see it from
a fresh perspective or to try to see it consistently from a
perspective which has already been glimpsed. My study
attempts this latter task by moving again and again from
Milton's lyrical prologues to the poem's narrative proper.
In a lesser work than *Paradise Lost* such a narrow point
of entry might well confine one to the outskirts without
ever allowing real access to the poem's center. But the
structure of *Paradise Lost* is such that almost any by-path
leads eventually to the main road, and I hope to demonstrate here that in fact to understand Milton's conception
of the Christian poet is finally to travel a long way toward
understanding the essential argument of Milton's epic.
Moreover, my particular approach to Milton's poem has,
I think, certain distinct strengths. By looking at the narrative of *Paradise Lost* with an eye to its particular significance for the poet, Milton, we can achieve an increased
awareness of the power of a single great mind not only,
as some have insisted, handing down a dogmatic system
of values but also considering the distinct possibilities
offered to man as responses to his world.

Surely for an age uncertain of its moral imperatives,
the final relevance of *Paradise Lost* lies in what it can

tell us of how *this* man—a man of intelligence, learning, broad imaginative scope, and wide experience of the world—comprehended the possibilities of being human. By looking at Milton's epic from the poet's angle of vision we can dispel Dr. Johnson's impression that "the want of human interest is always felt."[19]

[19] Johnson, IX, 152.

1: The Poet and Satan

A FAMILIAR group of Milton's readers have not shared Adam's confidence that "Evil into the mind of God or Man / May come and go, so unapprov'd, and leave / No spot or blame behind" (V, 117–119); they have instead assumed, less charitably, that the impact of Satan's character in *Paradise Lost* implies an uncomprehended diabolical complicity on the part of the poet. Such readings have been vigorously rebutted,[1] but they manage to persist because they respond with appealing directness to what can hardly be missed: Satan is impressive. He impresses not just the romantic imagination and its offshoots; in seventeenth-century England the appeal of his heroics would have touched any admirer of Achilles or Hector or Aeneas. Of course most of Milton's first audience would have been willing, ultimately, to accept the poet's stated assessment of Satan's heroism, whereas Shelley, for instance, was not. But precisely because Milton's early readers knew the Devil was bad and did not, like C. S. Lewis, have to prove it, they could respond more

[1] Prominent voices here are C. S. Lewis, *A Preface to "Paradise Lost"* (London: Oxford Univ. Press, 1942) and Douglas Bush, *'Paradise Lost' in Our Time* (New York: Peter Smith, 1957).

openly to his admirable qualities, to his suffering fortitude and constancy of purpose.

   Much post-Romantic criticism has lost this sense of
balance and has viewed *Paradise Lost* partially. Milton
clearly intends to condemn Satan (who could doubt it?),
but he just as clearly provides materials for the Satanist
critique—a critique which offers us valuable intuitions:
"Milton . . . was a true poet and of the Devil's party without knowing it."[2] Blake's notorious claim not only helps
to suggest the complexity of Milton's struggle with evil;
it also serves to isolate an important dimension of *Paradise Lost* by insisting that Milton's relation as poet to
the structure he created is a primary concern and that, in
particular, the relation of the poet to Satan is crucial.
These are important considerations, but they remain dis-
torted in Blake and those who subsequently have shared
his attitude toward the place of Satan in Milton's poem.
The reason for this distortion is plain: the Satanists, almost without exception, presume to know more than
Milton about the workings of the creative imagination.
will be arguing that so to presume is usually to ignore the
information Milton offers us concerning his own creative
process. In his characterization of Satan, Milton leaves
us little room for second-guessing about his unconscious
sympathies. His poem demonstrates an acute sensitivity
to both the appeals and the dangers of Satanism; his
imagination is not covertly inflamed by fallen grandeur.
In short, Milton knew exactly to what extent he was "of
the Devil's party." In his epic he anticipates the Satanist

   [2] William Blake, *The Marriage of Heaven and Hell* in *The
Complete Writings of William Blake*, ed., Geoffrey Keynes (Oxford: The Clarendon Press, 1966), p. 150.

response by repeatedly asking us to compare his portrait of the poet with his portrait of Satan. The similarities are not hidden; the differences are consciously and carefully defined.

Denis Saurat has told us that "Milton had Satan in him and wanted to drive him out."[3] This is a blunt way to put things, but Saurat would be close to the truth if he did not also insist that Milton was unaware of his potential Satanism—in particular that he was unaware of the potentially satanic aspect of his aspiration to so great a work as *Paradise Lost.* When in Book II we discover Satan poised on the brink of Hell contemplating his flight into Chaos, his "thoughts inflamed of Highest design" (II, 630), or when we are told that Satan, "Thus high uplifted beyond hope, aspires / Beyond thus high" (II, 7–8), we should not shy away from recalling the poet at the outset desiring "with no middle flight . . . to soar / Above th' *Aonian* Mount" (I, 14–15). Or again, when in Book I we hear Satan's proud self-justification, "till then who knew / The force of those dire Arms?" (I, 93–94), and later find him once more willing to face an "unknown Region . . . / Unknown dangers" (II, 443–444), we should not, in supposed deference to the forgetful poet, refuse to recollect his initial aspiration to try the unknown and achieve "Things unattempted yet" (I, 16). We should not, in short, smugly assume that Milton was missing the potential irony of such comparisons. By means of echoes like these he intends us to ask a question, a question he himself was, I think, the first to ask: is the attempt to write *Paradise Lost* presumptuous? Milton answers, "Yes,

[3] *Milton, Man and Thinker* (New York: Dial Press, 1925), p. 220.

'I have presum'd, / An Earthly Guest, and drawn Empyreal Air' " (VII, 13–14); his constant hope, however, is that the risk he runs is not prompted by self-justifying and self-inflating pride.

In the invocation to Book I Milton's poet announces his subject, "Man's First Disobedience" (I, 1), and proceeds directly to exalt its importance—to make clear from the outset the audacity of his attempt to explain to fallen men the justice of God's ways. He calls to a heavenly muse:

> *. . . I thence*
> *Invoke thy aid to my advent'rous Song,*
> *That with no middle flight intends to soar*
> *Above th' Aonian Mount, while it pursues*
> *Things unattempted yet in Prose or Rhyme.*
>   (I, 12–16)

There is no quibbling with greatness here. Milton is probably echoing Ariosto, who at the beginning of *Orlando Furioso* had proudly invoked not a heavenly muse but his own mistress.[4] By ranking himself beside the Italian poet, Milton may ultimately intend a contrast: like Adam, Ariosto hearkened to the promptings of a mortal woman; the poet of *Paradise Lost* looks to higher authority. Initially, however, the allusion serves simply to recall Ariosto's haughty tone ("I make no doubt but

---

[4] The "things unattempted yet" topos has a long history, for a summary of which see Ernst Robert Curtius, *European Literature and the Latin Middle Ages*, trans. Willard Trask (New York: Pantheon Books, 1953), pp. 85–86. Milton was surely aware of this tradition, as he was also undoubtedly aware that his most recent significant predecessor in the use of this topos was Ariosto. See Hughes' note to I, 16 and IX, 29–31 of *Paradise Lost*.

I shall have the skill / As much as I have promised to fulfill"),[5] and thereby to emphasize the hint of hubris latent throughout the first prologue to *Paradise Lost*. Less than twenty-five lines after this ambitious beginning Milton's epic voice sings of Satan:

> *. . . with all his Host*
> *Of Rebel Angels, by whose aid aspiring*
> *To set himself in Glory above his Peers,*
> *He trusted to have equall'd the most High. . . .*
> > *Him the Almighty Power*
> *Hurl'd headlong flaming from th' Ethereal Sky*
> *With hideous ruin and combustion down*
> *to bottomless perdition.*
>
> > (I, 37–47)

The immediate juxtaposition of the soaring ascent anticipated by the poet with the precipitous fall of the rebel angels suggests, at least, that Milton saw potential in his own circumstances as aspiring singer of divine epic the consequences of Satan's "ambitious aim." In viewing Satan and his cohorts we shall see this suggestion continually reinforced—for example, in the fall of Mulciber at the end of Book I. Here, specifically, an architect of things divine is cast down for his share in satanic overreaching.

The initial invocation is not, of course, a cry of rebellion but a call for divine assistance:

> *What in me is dark*
> *Illumine, what is low raise and support;*
> *That to the highth of this great Argument*

---

[5] Harington's translation.

I may assert Eternal Providence
And justify the ways of God to men.

(I, 22–26)

It should be clear that for Milton it is the poet's submission to the voice of his muse, to divine inspiration, which ultimately distinguishes the soaring creation of *Paradise Lost* from an act of blasphemous pride. Milton does not, however, present the invocation of a heavenly muse as his only defense against presuming too much. Throughout the narrative he remains sensitive to the relation between himself as poet and his subject; he examines every implication of his creative act with a care which suggests a fear of self-delusion. While he insists on the pious intentions of what he undertakes, he never neglects to expose the satanic aspect of his poetic posture.

II

The mechanism of the poet's inspiration is based on a paradoxical pattern of outward darkness and inward illumination. In the prologue to Book III, Milton employs this paradox to express not only his humble dependence on God's grace but also the weakness and corresponding audacity of his presumptuous adventure beyond his own "Diurnal Sphere." Like fallen Satan, throwing round "his balefull eyes" (I, 56) in Hell, the poet, a fallen man, dwells in darkness:

> . . . *but thou [Light]*
> *Revisit'st not these eyes, that roll in vain*
> *To find thy piercing ray, and find no dawn;*
> *So thick a drop serene hath quencht thir Orbs,*
> *Or dim suffusion veil'd.*

(III, 22–26)

To aim high from the depths of such obscurity is to echo Satan's despairing boast:

> *From this descent*
> *Celestial Virtues rising, will appear*
> *More glorious and more dread than from no fall.*
>
> (II, 14–16)[6]

Throughout his prologues, the poet, "In darkness, and with dangers compast round" (VII, 27), repeatedly emphasizes the baseness of his condition; such an emphasis cannot exclude an awareness of the similarity between the poet's physical circumstances and those of his epic villain whose dwelling place is measured by its distance from light.[7] Indeed, in his second invocation Milton insists on this similarity by placing his narrator in a posture much more broadly reminiscent of Satan:

> *Thee [holy Light] I revisit now with bolder wing,*
> *Escap't the* Stygian *Pool, though long detain'd*
> *In that obscure sojourn, while in my flight*
> *Through utter and through middle darkness borne*
> *With other notes than to th'* Orphean Lyre
> *I sung of* Chaos *and* Eternal Night. . . .
>
> (III, 13–18)

This passage follows *directly* the conclusion of Book II—over one hundred lines describing Satan's escape from Hell and labored flight up through Chaos. There is a

---

[6] This also imitates the pattern of paradox inherent in the fortunate fall. Milton continually shows us that the shape of good can be imitated by evil.

[7] Note Sin's description of Hell: "With terrors and with clamors compasst round" (II, 862). In addition to being "In darkness and with dangers compast round" (VII, 27), the poet is plagued by "the barbarous dissonance / Of Bacchus and his Revellers" (VII, 32–33).

sense, of course, in which the epic narrator must trace Satan's journey in order to describe it. But to take pains to visualize both the narrator and Satan struggling through "this wild Abyss / The Womb of nature" (II, 910–911)—Satan "Audacious" (II, 931), the poet "with bolder wing"—achieves nothing so much as to suggest an analogy between the two daring voyagers. The analogy is not simply glimpsed; Milton develops it in detail.

Just as the poet in the prologue to Book III has labored out of darkness to win the visionary illumination bestowed by God, so Satan's flight in Book II through the "darksome Desert" of Chaos is directed toward light. As the arch Fiend approaches the Sun, his "visual ray" is

> . . . *sharp'n'd* . . .
> *To Objects distant far, whereby he soon*
> *Saw within ken a glorious Angel stand,*
> *The same whom* John *saw also in the Sun.*
>   (III, 620–623)

The poet has, at the beginning of this book, applied to holy Light for direction and increased clarity that he might "see and tell / Of things invisible to mortal sight" (III, 54–55). So here Satan, "Alone, thus wand'ring" (III, 667), applies to the Regent of the Sun, Uriel, for assistance in his anticreative task. His formal address to Uriel is an unmistakable, though bombastic, echo of a Miltonic invocation:

> Uriel, *for thou of those sev'n Spirits that stand*
> *In sight of God's high Throne, gloriously bright,*
> *The first art wont his great authentic will*
> *Interpreter through highest Heav'n to bring,*
> *Where all his Sons thy Embassy attend;*

> *And here art likeliest by supreme decree*
> *Like honor to obtain, and as his Eye*
> *To visit oft this new Creation round . . . .*
> > *Brightest Seraph, tell*
> *In which of all these shining Orbs hath Man*
> *His fixed seat, or fixed seat hath none*
> *But all these shining Orbs his choice to dwell;*
> *That I may find him, and with secret gaze,*
> *Or open admiration him behold. . . .*
> > (III, 654–672)

Satan, dissembling, does not simply adopt the supplicating posture of the poet: while his rhetoric is inflated and his periods suspended beyond anything the poet, speaking for himself, attempts, still the content and syntactic formulas of Satan's speech distinctly recall the voice of the poet invoking his muse. Satan's request for heavenly guidance ("Brightest Seraph, tell") is, of course, the keynote of Milton's first invocation ("Instruct me, for Thou know'st. . . . Say first" [I, 19, 27]). The compound string of eulogistic epithet and description through which Satan ingratiates himself with Uriel and Satan's cautious offering of alternatives ("In which . . . hath Man / His fixed seat, or fixed seat hath none / . . . with secret gaze, / Or open admiration") looks back to the beginning of Book III and the poet's address to Light:

> *Hail holy Light, offspring of Heav'n first-born*
> *Or of th'Eternal Coeternal beam*
> *May I express thee unblam'd? since God is Light,*
> *And never but in unapproached Light*
> *Dwelt from Eternity, dwelt then in thee*
> *Bright effluence of bright essence increat.*
> > (III, 1–6)

Again in Book VII we find a similar suspended list of
heavenly qualities and a similar offering of alternatives
which here place Urania, like Uriel, "In sight of God's
high Throne":

> *Descend from Heav'n* Urania, *by that name*
> *If rightly thou art call'd . . . .*
>   *for thou*
> *Nor of the Muses nine, nor on the top*
> *Of old* Olympus *dwell'st, but Heav'nly born.*
> *Before the Hills appear'd, or Fountain flow'd,*
> *Thou with Eternal Wisdom didst converse,*
> *Wisdom thy Sister, and with her didst play*
> *In presence of th' Almighty Father. . . .*
>
>   (VII, 1–11)

Before the powers of heavenly instruction Satan, in his
manner, resembles the poet, a humble servant of God—
a resemblance good enough to fool Uriel. The likeness
between the two is further suggested by the fact that
Uriel, to whom the Devil looks for aid, shares with the
poet's muse ("Thou from the first / Wast present" [I,
19–20]) special knowledge of the Creation: "I saw when
at his Word the formless mass / This world's material
mould, came to a heap" (III, 708–709). These multiple
similarities do not seem random. That both Satan and
the poet seek, in syntactically echoing passages, assistance from light and from sources of hexaemeral knowledge should appear striking. It should make clear that
Milton is looking at the poet's situation in terms of Satan's fallen posture and wishes to communicate this perspective. The question, to repeat, is why Milton invites
such a comparison, and the answer, again, is that recog-

nizing the audacity of his own high poetic aspirations he wishes to distinguish them clearly from the kind of aspiring he sees as satanic. He is after the contrast, but he does not wish to gain it by slighting the similarities. On the contrary, the more clearly he can see and project the similarities between the poet and Satan, the more sure he can be that he has not been blinded by pride.

The crucial contrast is obvious but significant in that Milton employs it to speak for himself. Satan, unlike the poet, is lying. Uriel is persuaded to think that the Devil's purposes are exactly opposite to what they really are:

> *Fair Angel, thy desire which tends to know*
> *The works of God, thereby to glorify*
> *The great Work-Master*, leads to no excess
> That reaches blame, but rather merits praise
> The more it seems excess. . . .
>
> (III, 694–698; my emphasis.)

The glorification of God is not what Satan has in mind, but it is precisely what the poet sees as the province of his own attempt. For the poet what "seems excess"—the attempt to discover "things invisible to mortal sight"—will, he hopes, "merit praise." Milton here seizes the occasion of the Devil's lie to define his own purposes.

Milton's use of Satan's stance as a foil to the poet's position is perhaps made most explicit at the beginning of Book IV. Here the Fiend, having landed on "Niphates top," turns his gaze toward Heaven and speaks directly to the Sun. The speech is a rough inversion and travesty of Milton's familiar "Hail holy Light":

> *O thou that with surpassing Glory crown'd*
> *Look'st from thy sole Dominion like the God*
> *Of this new World; at whose sight all the Stars*
> *Hide thir diminisht heads; to thee I call,*
> *But with no friendly voice, and add thy name*
> *O Sun, to tell thee how I hate thy beams*
> *That bring to my remembrance from what state*
> *I fell, how glorious once above thy Sphere:*
> *Till Pride and worse Ambition threw me down.*
>   (IV,32–41)

The poet and the Devil again, in a warped glass, reflect each other, and latent in the fact that Milton's hymn to holy Light can be subjected to satanic parody is the suggestion that hubristic presumption lies close to the surface of the second invocation. But the poet has hesitated: "May I express thee unblamed?" Perhaps he may. In the most obvious sense the comparable addresses to light serve emphatically to demonstrate the difference between the poet and the Apostate. While the poet asks for assistance, humbles himself before holy Light, prays, Satan hurls envious defiance at a lesser luminary.

III

Basic to this comparison of the poet and Satan is a symbolic use of place and posture in which, as I have been suggesting, physical circumstances often have clear moral equivalents. That Milton frequently allows movement and placement to suggest moral states is easy to see and has often been noticed: Hell is a place as are Heaven and Eden; to sin is to fall. One particular aspect of this equation of the spacial and the moral in which recent critics

have shown interest is Milton's use of the verb *wander*.
Isabel MacCaffrey, for one, documents the fact that "Not
only moral values, but the intellectual values on which
they depend, can be objectified, in Milton's topography,
by the identification of physical and spiritual 'wandering.'
Error is the linking word."[8] I have already cited Satan
describing to Uriel his erratic and malicious voyage
through Chaos, "Alone thus wand'ring." MacCaffrey
lists additional instances of Milton's use of the verb,
such as his description of the wandering pilgrims who
sought Christ in Golgotha (III, 476–477), Adam's warning against "wand'ring thoughts, and notions vaine"
(VIII, 187), Eve's recognition of loss ("From thee / How
shall I part, and whither wander down / Into a lower
World" [XI, 281–283]), and the poignant "wand'ring
steps and slow," which completes Milton's picture of our
fallen parents. Clearly *wander* is one of the several words
in *Paradise Lost* to which the reader becomes sensitized
through repetition. Recently Stanley Fish has added to
MacCaffrey's list and has warned us against the attempt
to read *wander* the same way in different contexts. The
relevance of context to meaning is, of course, crucial,
but with a word used as Milton uses *wander*, repetition
tends to encourage a comparison of the very contexts
within which the word appears. Discriminations, such
as can be made, are the result of these comparisons.[9]

[8] *"Paradise Lost" as "Myth"* (Cambridge, Mass.: Harvard Univ.
Press, 1959), p. 190.
[9] See *Surprised by Sin* (New York: St. Martin's Press, 1967), pp.
130–141. More recently in "Discovery as Form in *Paradise Lost*,"
New Essays on "Paradise Lost," Thomas Kranidas, ed. (Berkeley:
Univ. of California Press, 1969), pp. 1–14, Fish also writes, "When
the reader comes across a word or a phrase that recalls him to an

What interests me here about *wander* is that it serves
to relate the poet of the prologues to the characters of
Milton's narrative. What we learn of the word in the
poem proper lends a sense of human helplessness to the
lyrical lines:

> *Yet not the more*
> *Cease I to wander where the Muses haunt*
> *Clear Spring, or shady Grove, or Sunny Hill,*
> *Smit with the love of sacred Song. . . .*
>   (III, 26–29)[10]

Everywhere in the prologues Milton's description of the
poet's creative song is seen metaphorically as a journey—
a dark descent, a soaring flight. This spatial sense of
human activity is, of course, informed by the Puritan
preachers' favorite image of the Christian life: the wayfaring pilgrim, seeking Heaven, directed by light. As the
pilgrims "stray'd so farr . . . / In Golgotha" remind us,
such wayfaring was full of perils for frail humanity. In
the prologue to Book VII Milton repeats the word *wander*
to relate these perils specifically to the poet whose journey
passes dangerously near the abyss of satanic aspiration:

---

earlier point in the poem, he is not being asked to compare the
contents of two scenes now juxtaposed in his mind, but to apply
whatever insights he has gained in the *psychological* interim to
the single content these two scenes share" (p. 7). This looks like
a point of difference between Fish and myself, but I think we are
not so very far apart. I certainly agree with what seems to be the
central issue: that parallels in *Paradise Lost* exist not as ends in
themselves but, to repeat, as means to the forcing of distinctions,
distinctions the poet makes and the reader should also be making.

[10] For a similar comment on these lines see Anne Davidson
Ferry, *Milton's Epic Voice* (Cambridge, Mass.: Harvard Univ.
Press, 1963), p. 41.

> *Up led by thee [Urania]*
> *Into the Heav'n of Heav'ns I have presum'd*
> *An Earthly Guest, and drawn Empyreal Air,*
> *Thy temp'ring; with like safety guided down*
> *Return me to my Native Element:*
> *Lest from this flying Steed unrein'd, (as once*
> Bellerophon, *though from a lower Clime)*
> *Dismounted on th'* Aleian *Field I fall*
> *Erroneous there to wander and forlorn.*
> (VII, 12–20)

Here the poet wishes to avoid the erroneous wandering of a Bellerophon (a type of Satan) by means of celestial assistance.[11] He asks Urania that he be "led" and "guided" in his epic wayfaring. The request parallels Satan's plea for assistance during his wandering flight through Chaos:

> *Ye Powers*
> *And Spirits of this nethermost Abyss*
> Chaos *and* ancient Night, *I come no Spy,*
> *With purpose to explore or to disturb*
> *The secrets of your Realm, but by constraint*

[11] See J. B. Broadbent, *Some Graver Subject: An Essay on "Paradise Lost"* (London: Chatto and Windus, 1960), p. 235: "but why Bellerophon? It can only be because the invocation intrudes into the poem's structure the poet's anxiety about the presumptuous heroics of Book VI and the cosmography of Books VII and VIII. Bellerophon insures Milton against the sin of Adam and Eve, curiosity." See also Joseph H. Summers, *The Muse's Method* (Cambridge, Mass.: Harvard Univ. Press, 1962), p. 137: "The poet contrasts his own presumption in composing what we have read thus far with Satan's; but he faces the possibility that he may fall, to wander in madness like Bellerophon, if divine wisdom does not attend him in his descent to our 'Native Element.'"

> *Wand'ring this darksome Desert, as my way*
> *Lies through your spacious Empire up to light,*
> *Alone, and without guide, half lost, I seek*
> *What readiest path leads where your gloomy*
>   *bounds*
> *Confine with Heav'n; or if some other place*
> *From your Dominion won, th' Ethereal King*
> *Possesses lately, thither to arrive*
> *I travel this profound, direct my course.*
>   (II, 968–980)

These passages, taken together, serve again to emphasize the difference between Satan's mission to falsify God's ways to man and Milton's task. In his attempt at ordered poetic creation Milton's epic voice directs its request to Heaven, the ultimate source of all creation; Satan, on the other hand, intending to destroy, to "Erect the Standard . . . of *ancient Night*" (II, 986), where God has built, applies for guidance to disorder itself.

It should by now be clear that in depicting Satan's effort to subvert God's providential ways Milton continually reminds us of the poet's own activity. In the description related by the epic voice, Satan's intention of beguiling mankind initially appears—not just to the devils—as an immense undertaking "Of hazard" (II, 453, 455). To the infernal host Satan's destructive journey is "th' adventure" (II, 474), Satan "their great adventurer" (X, 440); and when the Devil himself describes his "adventure hard" (X, 468) we are surely meant to recall that the poet's own voyaging in Hell and Heaven is "advent'rous" (I, 13). Yet here, so the poet hopes, the similarity ends. "Whom shall we find / Sufficient" (II, 403–404), Beëlzebub asks, and Satan answers, "this en-

terprise / None shall partake with me" (II, 465–466).
The Devil continually deludes himself about his own self-sufficiency; in action he hopes to succeed through individual "strength," "art," and "evasion" (II, 410–411).
The poet, by contrast, is weak ("fall'n on evil days / On evil days though fall'n, and evil tongues" [VII, 25–26]), artless ("my unpremeditated Verse" [IX, 24]), and completely open concerning the possibilities, dangers, and intentions of his song. While the poet aspires to "no middle flight," he is ultimately dependent for support on divine inspiration; the Devil, attempting "solitary flight" (II, 632), benightedly convinces himself that he is "self-begot, self-rais'd" (V, 860). In describing Mammon's proposal to found an empire in Hell after the pattern of Heaven the epic voice gives us the phrase which exactly describes the kind of comparison Milton is attempting between poet and devil: "emulation opposite" (II, 298).

IV

The ways in which the poet of *Paradise Lost* "emulates" the devils may at first glance appear puzzling. Take, for example, a small detail from Book I—Satan's rousing of his troops from the burning lake:

> *Yet to thir General's Voice they soon obey'd*
> *Innumerable. As when the potent Rod*
> *Of* Amram's *Son in* Egypt's *evil day*
> *Wav'd round the Coast, up call'd a pitchy cloud*
> *Of* Locusts, *warping on the Eastern Wind,*
> *That o'er the Realm of impious* Pharaoh *hung*
> *Like Night, and darken'd all the Land of* Nile.
>
> (I, 337–343)

In the standard Christian typology which controls most of *Paradise Lost*, Satan is placed at the head of a list of villains which prominently includes Pharaoh, not his opposite, Moses. But here it is primarily *"Amram's* Son" with whom Satan is compared—"That Shepherd, who first taught the chosen Seed, / In the Beginning how the Heav'ns and Earth / Rose out of Chaos" (I, 8–10)—that shepherd with whom Milton has compared the poet at the beginning of Book I. It should appear initially odd that Milton employs the figure of Moses to describe both the poet and the Devil. It should appear odd, that is, until it becomes clear that Milton is consistently laboring to place poet and devil in comparable contexts. For Milton the shape of good and evil could be paradoxically similar; both Moses *and* Pharaoh could, superficially, resemble Satan, as they do in this passage if we look at it closely. Not only does Satan, in summoning his fallen cohorts, appear as Moses calling forth the plague of locusts; he also resembles here his proper type, Pharaoh, in that the plague he calls forth, while it descends on a land of captivity, descends at the same time on his own land. The devils are both slaves and masters, both seraphic lords and locusts (a standard analogy);[12] they are their own Hell. This doubleness of reference with respect to Satan and the devils is picked up within a few lines and emphasized:

> *Till, as a signal giv'n, th'uplifted Spear*
> *Of thir great Sultan waving to direct*
> *Thir course, in even balance down they light* . . . .
>   (I, 347–349)

[12] The analogy is based on Revelation 9: 1–6.

While the uplifted spear of Satan continues to resemble the "potent Rod / Of *Amram's* Son," the appellation "great Sultan" simultaneously identifies the Devil with Moses' enemy, Pharaoh. The complexity of Milton's use of allusion here corresponds to his attitude toward the infernal host. The devils are not simply monstrous. They incorporate and reflect (and, of course, pervert) the world's magnificence, even, in shadowing the chosen seed, its blessedness.

William Empson has provided some lively commentary on the similarity between diabolic attitudes and the attitudes of men of virtue as Milton saw them. Empson quotes Satan's address to the rebel forces in Book V:

> *Thrones, Dominations, Princedoms, Virtues,*
> *   Powers,*
> *If these magnific Titles yet remain*
> *Not merely titular. . . .*
>
> *Will ye submit your necks, and choose to bend*
> *The supple knee? ye will not, if I trust*
> *To know ye right, or if ye know yourselves*
> *Natives and Sons of Heav'n possest before*
> *By none, and if not equal all yet free,*
> *Equally free; for Orders and Degrees*
> *Jar not with liberty, but well consist.*
> *Who can in reason then or right assume*
> *Monarchy over such as live by right*
> *His equals, if in power and splendor less,*
> *In freedom equal? or can introduce*
> *Law and Edict on us, who without law*
> *Err not? Much less for this to be our Lord,*

> *And look for adoration to th' abuse*
> *Of those Imperial Titles which assert*
> *Our being ordain'd to govern, not to serve?*
> (V, 772–774; 787–802)

It is startling to come to this passage directly from a reading of Milton's prose controversy. Not only does Satan argue, like the republican Milton, from a position which couples native liberty with an insistence on degree and discipline; in writing this speech Milton could hardly have escaped hearing the accents of his own voice:

Is it such an unspeakable joy to serve, such felicity to wear a yoke, to clink our shackles locked on by pretended law of subjection, more intolerable and hopeless to be ever shaken off than those which are knocked on by illegal injury and violence?[13]

I find both in our own and foreign story, that dukes, earls, and marquises were at first not hereditary, not empty and vain titles, but names of trust and office; and with the office ceasing, as induces me to be of opinion that every worthy man in parliament . . . might for the public good be thought a fit peer and judge of the king. . . . Whence doubtless our ancestors, who were not ignorant with what rights either nature or ancient constitution had endowed them . . . thought it no way illegal to depose and put to death their tyrannous kings.[14]

Empson's estimate of the effect of Satan's republicanism on Milton's contemporaries should make any fair-minded reader pause:

[13] *The Ready and Easy Way to Establish a Free Commonwealth* (C.E., VI, 136).

[14] *The Tenure of Kings and Magistrates* (C.E., V, 25).

Surely the first readers must have found this intriguing; the only good writer who had defended the regicide was ascribing to the devils the sentiments still firmly held by himself and his proscribed party. They would not find the speech particularly dull and cooked-up, as Mr. Eliot did; and they would not be at all sure how far the author meant the devil's remarks to be wrong.[15]

Empson is not concerned so much with the inconsistency of Milton's politics (they are not inconsistent here) as with the unattractiveness of his theology. He quite clearly sees the trouble with Satan's rebellion, which is, of course, that Satan is not simply opposing a "King anointed" (V, 777), an absolute monarch "upheld by old repute, / Consent or custom" (I, 639–640); he is rebelling against God, the source of all degree, a nonauthoritarian, immanent deity.[16] What is interesting about Empson's exposition is that he displays broadly what no reader should miss: the subject of *Paradise Lost* is rebellion, rebellion faulted by an author who was himself for his own and subsequent ages a prime spokesman for "the good old Cause." Typically, Milton did not attempt to disguise this seeming paradox. Schooled in rebellion, he openly granted the Devil the advantage of what he had learned in defense of liberty. I am not as sure as Empson that Milton's contemporaries would have been confused as to "how far the author meant the devil's remarks to be wrong," but I think it undeniable that the politics of Hell are an instance of Milton's concern to demonstrate, both to his readers and to himself, how close in fact he was to a Satanic position.

[15] William Empson, *Milton's God* (London: Chatto and Windus, 1961), p. 82.
[16] Empson, p. 75.

Other instances of the poet's proximity to Satanism occur in Book II—particularly in the passage describing Hell's Olympian games:

> *Others more milde,*
> *Retreated in a silent valley, sing*
> *With notes Angelical to many a Harp*
> *Thir own Heroic deeds and hapless fall*
> *By doom of Battle; and complain that Fate*
> *Free Virtue should enthrall to Force or Chance.*
>
> *Others apart sat on a Hill retir'd,*
> *In thoughts more elevate, and reason'd high*
> *Of Providence, Foreknowledge, Will, and Fate,*
> *Fixt Fate, Free will, Foreknowledge absolute,*
> *And found no end in wand'ring mazes lost.*
> *Of good and evil much they argu'd then,*
> *Of happiness and final misery. . . .*
>
> (II, 546–551; 557–563)

Dennis Burden is the most recent critic to observe that "this intellectual and poetic Hell is something with which the poem is deeply concerned."[17] The poets of Hell sing epic ("Thir own Heroic deeds") and tragedy ("complain that Fate / Free Virtue should enthrall to Force or Chance");[18] the infernal philosophers reason "high / Of Providence, Foreknowledge, Will, and Fate"; and the song

[17] *The Logical Epic* (Cambridge, Mass.: Harvard Univ. Press, 1967), p. 58.

[18] See Howard Schultz, *Milton and Forbidden Knowledge* (New York: MLA Revolving Fund Series, 17, 1955), p. 90. In a discussion of the passage similar to Burden's, Schultz assures us that Milton is referring to tragedy here by comparing lines 550–551 with *Paradise Regained*, IV, 261–266.

of the poet-philosopher, Milton, is crucially involved in all of this. While he aspires to sing Christian heroism, "argument / Not less but more Heroic than the wrath / Of stern Achilles" (IX, 13–15); while his tragic notes (IX, 6) are tempered by Providence, not ruled by Chance; and while his explanation of "Free Will" and "Foreknowledge absolute" is not, like the devils' speculation, cut off from God; still his consignment of the pagan precedents for his song to Hell argues for his willingness to expose how close his hoped-for light is to darkness. Burden's sense of Milton's mind is, I think, correct: Milton's experience in controversy made him instinctively seize upon the counterargument. He wished to encompass his adversary, not ignore him, and his encompassment of Satan made him fully aware of the seductions the satanic posture had for a mind such as his own.

V

Just as Milton allows the devils to engage in something like his own poetic activity, so too he is willing to lay bare the dangers latent in the fundamental source of this activity, his inspiration. The essential message of Milton's epic invocations is, to repeat, that everything, for the poet, depends upon his muse. The muse is both his support and justification. Such support, such justification is not commanded by the poet; rather it is sought by prayer, the efficacy of which must remain in doubt. Milton's final prologue in *Paradise Lost* ends with the fear that "all [may] be mine / Not Hers who brings it nightly to my Ear" (IX, 46–47). This tenuousness as to the sources and effectiveness of the poet's inspiration is often implicit in the poem's "argument," and one place in which such an implication can be found is in Milton's treatment of topography.

Inspiration in *Paradise Lost* is almost inevitably associated with a physical setting. Milton's sense of place in this is traditional: he selects mountains and neighboring woods and waters as the sites of inspirational vision. His classical precedents for such settings, which he names outright or suggests by description, are the haunts of the Homeric muses: "th' *Aonian* Mount" (I, 15), "th' *Olympian* Hill" (VII, 3), and the Castalian Spring on Mount Parnassus (III, 28). Yet while he does not cease "to wander where the Muses haunt / Clear Spring, or shady Grove, or Sunny Hill" (III, 27–28), he wishes to soar above "th' *Olympian* Hill" and therefore prefers the biblical counterparts to these places of inspiration. He calls the Mosaic Muse "Of *Oreb* or of *Sinai*" (I, 7) and the spirit dwelling in "*Sion* and th' flowery Brooks beneath" (III, 30).

"*Sion* Hill / ... and *Siloa's* Brook" (I, 10–11) represent for Milton and his Christian contemporaries archetypal settings for the manifestations of God's grace. In Book III Satan views "Direct against" the magnificent stairs which Jacob will see ascending to Heaven

> *A passage down to th' Earth, a passage wide,*
> *Wider by far than that of after-times*
> *Over Mount Sion, and, though that were large,*
> *Over the Promis'd Land to God so dear,*
> *By which, to visit oft those happy Tribes,*
> *On high behests his Angels to and fro*
> *Pass'd frequent. ...*
>
> (III, 528–534)

As these lines suggest, Sion Hill, on which David built his altar, Solomon, the Temple, constituted in Milton's traditional thought a focal point of communication between man and God.[19] In *Paradise Lost* we frequently see types of Sion Hill: Mount Sinai is clearly one; in respect to inspiration Milton seems to have considered Olympus and Parnassus pagan shadows of God's holy hill; Michael, descending from Heaven to instruct fallen Adam,

> ... *on a Hill made halt*
> *A glorious Apparition, had not doubt*
> *And carnal fear that day dimm'd* Adam's *eye.*
> *Not that more glorious, when the Angels met*
> Jacob *in* Mahanaim, *where he saw*
> *The field Pavilion'd with his Guardians bright;*
> *Nor that which on the flaming Mount appear'd*
> *In* Dothan, *cover'd with a Camp of Fire*
> *Against the* Syrian *King. . . .*
>
> (XI, 210–218)

To administer Adam's vision of the future, the archangel ascends with our first father "a Hill / Of Paradise the highest" (XI, 377–378), and Raphael, sent by God to instruct unfallen men, alights upon "th' Eastern cliff of Paradise" (V, 275) itself a promontory from which our fallen parents must "wander down / Into a lower World" (XI, 282–283).

Paradise, of course, is not simply one of the fair dwelling places of God. It is also the site of Satan's fatal deception. Similarly the mount of speculation on which Adam learns from Michael "the sum / Of wisdom" (XII,

[19] See as an instance of Milton's typological reading of Sion, his translation of Psalm 84 in which Sion is portrayed as the first among God's "dwellings fair."

575–576) is compared by Milton to a place of satanic temptation:

> *Not higher that Hill nor wider looking round,*
> *Whereon for different cause the Tempter set*
> *Our second Adam in the Wilderness,*
> *To show him all the Earth's kingdoms and thir*
>   *Glory.*
>
>   (XI, 381–384)

If we look back at the roll call of devils in Book I, it becomes clear that this double aspect—sacred and profane —consistently characterizes Milton's conception of the places of inspiration. In such settings men have heard infernal as well as heavenly voices:

> *The chief were those who from the Pit of Hell*
> *Roaming to seek thir prey on earth, durst fix*
> *Thir Seats long after next the Seat of God,*
> *Thir Altars by his Altar, Gods ador'd*
> *Among the Nations round, and durst abide*
> Jehovah *thund'ring out of* Sion, *thron'd*
> *Between the Cherubim; yea, often plac'd*
> *Within his Sanctuary itself thir Shrines,*
> *Abominations; and with cursed things*
> *His holy Rites, and solemn Feasts profan'd*
> *And with thir darkness durst affront his light.*
>
>   (I, 381–391)

From Sion Hill itself, a dwelling place of the poet's muse, Milton moves to its environs and in so doing continues to convey the impression that divine inspiration can be confused with abomination by the unwary:

> *Nor content with such*
> *Audacious neighborhood, the wisest heart*
> *Of* Solomon *he [Moloch] led by fraud to build*
> *His Temple right against the Temple of God*
> *On that opprobrious Hill, and made his Grove*
> *The pleasant Valley of* Hinnom, Tophet *thence*
> *And black* Gehenna *call'd, the Type of Hell.*
>
> (I, 399–405)

Here "that opprobrious Hill," which appears twice more in the following fifty lines as "that Hill of scandal" (I, 416) and "th' offensive Mountain" (I, 443), is, strictly considered, Mount Olivet and represents, like Sion Hill, a frequently profaned site of God's condescension to men. (The "Hill of scandal" could in one sense actually be called Sion Hill since, for Milton, all Jerusalem's hills were the hills of Sion.)[20] The settings Milton associates with his Christian muse are further recalled in this passage by "the Type of Hell." A reader familiar with the geography of the Holy Land would notice that this same "pleasant Valley of *Hinnom*" is, as described by Jerome, "watered by the fountains of Siloam" (*In Jeremiam*, vii, 31)—by the "*Siloa*'s Brook" of Milton's initial invocation.[21] There is no real need to spend more time looking at a map of the Holy Land. My point is this: in the catalogue of devils Milton locates the fallen angels, emerged from Hell, in landmarks similar or identical to the places of inspiration mentioned by the poet at the beginning of

[20] For evidence of this see Milton's version of Psalm 87.

[21] See Allan H. Gilbert, *A Geographical Dictionary of Milton* (New Haven: Yale Univ. Press, 1919), p. 145. Gilbert believes that Milton's description of the valley as "pleasant" depends on Jerome.

Paradise Lost, and this placement suggests the dangers of hearkening to a voice speaking out of Sion. The poet runs a risk. Even the classical muses whom he refuses to ignore out of hand (III, 27–28; his debt to former epic is, he realizes, immense) are here emphatically consigned to Hell (I, 508–521).

It is, of course, true that Milton did not invent the geography of his infernal roll call, that his purpose was not simply to provide a contrasting echo to the landmarks of his first invocation. Nevertheless in his continued emphasis on the fact that the worship of God can be twisted and perverted into the adoration of Satan, he could hardly have missed the implication that the holiest of men must constantly be wary lest, blinded, their devotions degenerate to fume. The Devil was, in Milton's mind, constantly ready to deceive the proud man, and in this passage describing Sion's descent to idolatry, Milton's primary example of a man so deceived is Solomon "whose heart though large / Beguil'd by fair Idolatresses, fell / To Idols foul" (I, 444–446). I would like to suggest that the figure of Solomon had a particular exemplary significance for Milton. Solomon's name was, of course, associated with divine poetry, and Milton clearly saw himself as writing in the tradition of Sion's singers. At the same time Solomon's uxoriosness certainly represented for Milton— as both his life and his great epic testify—a crucial source of human error. But most significantly, I think, Solomon had built, under the guidance of God, the greatest religious monument of the Mosaic world, the Temple—a structure which, in medieval and Renaissance theories of artistic creation, constituted the ultimate model for all

artistic endeavor.[22] Solomon, building after the divinely
revealed fabric of God's world in "Measure, Number,
and Weight" (Wisdom of Solomon, 11:21), had served
for ages since Augustine as the archetypal example of the
human artist working in imitation of God's creative act.
Milton and his readers would not have missed the implication that, as a divinely inspired work, *Paradise Lost*
was obviously comparable both to the Temple and to the
world itself. Marvell, in his dedicatory poem, assumes
these analogies to be commonplace:

> *Thy verse created like thy theme sublime*
> *In Number, Weight, and Measure needs not Rime.*

Milton seems to be underscoring this connection between
Solomon and the poet when he emphasizes by repetition
that it was Solomon's "heart though large," his "wisest
heart" which was "led by fraud to build / His [Moloch's]
Temple right against the Temple of God." The emphasis
recalls the poet of the first invocation whose Muse prefers
"Before all Temples th' upright heart and pure" (I, 18).
While the poet is praying that his own heart will not be
deceived, "led by fraud," that he will not build an idolatrous temple, the example of Solomon remains before
him as a warning that those once confident of God's
blessing can still fall from grace.

[22] For discussions of the relevance of Solomon's Temple to
medieval and Renaissance theories of art see Curtius; Rudolf
Wittkower, *Architectural Principles in the Age of Humanism*
(London: Alec Tiranti, 1952); and Otto von Simson, *The Gothic
Cathedral* (New York: Pantheon Books, 1954). For an expanded
discussion of Satanic artistry as a parody of divine creativity see
Chapter IV, pp. 164–175.

While the example of Solomon's idolatrous building
casts a warning shadow over Milton's own "advent'rous"
(I, 13) attempt at a poetic monument to God, it also serves
as a mundane type of Hell's infernal arts—of Pandaemonium, "Built like a Temple" (I, 713) which far sur-
passes the world's "greatest Monuments of Fame, / And
Strength and Art" (I, 695–696), and of the "Advent'rous
work" (X, 255) undertaken by Sin and Death, the cause-
way from Hell, "a Monument / Of merit high" (X, 258–
259) which, like all infernal creations, parodies God's
own building in Chaos. In the case of Solomon's idolatrous works, we are dealing with an instance of human
history reflecting the play of forces and events in the
cosmos at large. Such a view of history was orthodox,
and, as many have recognized, such a view is central to
the unity of Milton's epic. In *Paradise Lost* Milton repeatedly exploits cosmic polarity to project on a grand
scale the predicament of man and the choices available
to him: man should, as one of the multitude of God's
creatures, obey the Almighty and magnify Him through
works; like a devil man may disobey God and fall, his
life and works then becoming dross for the hellhound
Death. The cosmic tensions of *Paradise Lost* reflect in
particular the situation of the poet who, as a member of
a fallen race, precariously attempts to counter the potential pride of his artistic aspirations with the humility
of selfless intentions and dependence on God. Viewed
with reference to the poet's own artistic predicament, the
examples of negative creativity which extend from Pandaemonium to the song which ravishes Hell (II, 546–555)
seem continually to suggest that the infernal aping of
heavenly artistry is dangerously similar to Milton's effort

in *Paradise Lost* to build, like Solomon, in imitation of the divine creative acts. I am arguing that the explicit comparisons of poet and devil in *Paradise Lost* are intended by Milton to demonstrate an undeluded recognition of the satanic potential of his poetic act. Within the epic, ambition and presumption dog the poet in the form of satanic resemblances to his attempt to understand and give poetic shape to the pattern of God's ways with men. But, by the very act of objectifying such resemblances in infernal analogies to the poet's aspiring flight, Milton is able to keep differences clearly in sight. When in Hell the devils ask, "As he our darkness, cannot we his Light / Imitate when we please?" (II, 269–270), an analogy to the poet's own undertaking is clearly in view. At the same time, however, the difference between poet and devil is here equally plain. The poet cannot imitate God's light *at will*. Like the earthly and heavenly opposites of sin— the prophets, the angels, the Son—Milton labors to express God's will, not his own. He rejects satanic self-sufficiency; he invokes the muse.

2: The Poet and Paradise

I

IN THE manner characteristic of Christian paradox, Milton's poem of paradise lost is a visionary prolegomenon to paradise found. Within the epic we are offered the lively image of our former perfection, and by the end we have been instructed that our regeneration consists not only in the comprehension of our loss but in the regaining of paradise by an inner possession of the edenic image. For the fit reader, *Paradise Lost* should begin an experience of recovery, an experience which finds its human center in the conception of paradise and in the drama of Eden.[1] In Eden we glimpse the pattern of what we might have been and what, in a new way, we may become; in Eden also lies a deadly warning, a tale of aspiration, temptation, and error which is exemplary for all of us and which, in a way peculiar to Milton's design, serves as a particular warning for our fallen representative within the poem—the poet.

[1] For discussion of paradise along these lines see in particular Louis L. Martz, *The Paradise Within* (New Haven: Yale Univ. Press, 1964); Stanley E. Fish, *Surprised by Sin* (New York: St. Martin's Press, 1967); and Northrop Frye, *The Return of Eden* (Toronto: Univ. of Toronto Press, 1965).

The extent to which the action of Eden can serve Milton as a relevant moral parable for postlapsarian men has been questioned directly or implicitly by those who insist too emphatically on a sharp, generic distinction between fallen and unfallen worlds. What, it is sometimes asked, can the golden dream of an effortless life tell us of the darkness and dangers of the world as we know it? How can a state of innocence inform men who must "[know] good by evil"? Such questions, as J. M. Evans has recently demonstrated in his valuable study of the Genesis tradition, are too often based on a misconception of the quality of Milton's paradise.[2] If we adopt the view that life in Milton's garden is simple, easy, placid, and (the usual corollary) boring, we will, to begin with, be forced to catch Milton in a number of obvious and awkward inconsistencies. For example, Raphael's injunction, "Solicit not thy thoughts to matters hid" (VIII, 167), must seem an authorial lapse to anyone who thinks the only real tension in Eden arises from that "Sole pledge of . . . obedience" (III, 95) concerning the forbidden tree. And what of Eve's wayward impulses or Adam's uxorious tendencies? Considerations such as these can readily move one along the road to the opposite extreme of concluding that Milton, wittingly or unwittingly, portrayed our first parents as fallen before they fell.[3] The

[2] J. M. Evans, *"Paradise Lost" and the Genesis Tradition* (Oxford: The Clarendon Press, 1968).

[3] See Millicent Bell's germinal article, "The Fallacy of the Fall in *Paradise Lost*," *PMLA*, 68 (1953), 863–883 and her exchange with Wayne Shumaker in *PMLA*, 70 (1955), 1185–1203. E. M. W. Tillyard's view of Adam and Eve's prelapsarian imperfection in *Studies in Milton* (London: Chatto and Windus, 1951) is similar to Mrs. Bell's. Also see H. V. S. Ogden's reply to both Bell and

answer to such difficulties resides in the view of Miltonic innocence offered by Evans:

> The whole point of Milton's description is that Man's innocence was not "effortless"; Adam and Eve's virtue was neither fugitive nor cloistered, and almost every episode in Books IV, V, and VIII is calculated to show that it was not. Throughout the poem Milton insists that on this earth perfection cannot be a condition of stability. The perfection of Adam and Eve no less than the perfection of the garden they inhabit is nothing if not conditional, for it requires their constant vigilance to preserve the balance of forces on which it depends.[4]

Like the luxuriant vegetation of Eden's native soil man's own natural impulses to growth must be controlled by a sense of limitation which is, in man, equally natural and resident in his powers of reason. God's prohibition, "This one, this easie charge," exists for Adam and Eve as "The only *sign* of our obedience" (IV, 421, 428; my emphasis), a "pledge" which both symbolizes man's maintenance of his middle state and creates the latitude within which man can, subject to his own restraints, innocently "please . . . [his] appetite / Though wand'ring"

Tillyard, "The Crisis of *Paradise Lost* Reconsidered," in *Milton: Modern Essays in Criticism*, Arthur E. Barker, ed. (New York: Oxford Univ. Press, 1965), pp. 308–327.

[4] Evans, p. 269. Evans argues convincingly that Milton employs imagery of vegetation to suggest an analogy between Adam and Eve's care of their physical garden and their keeping of their moral condition (see below). Almost simultaneously Barbara Kiefer Lewalski has presented a similar and equally convincing reading of Milton's paradise: "Innocence and Experience in Milton's Eden," *New Essays on "Paradise Lost,"* Thomas Kranidas, ed. (Berkeley: Univ. of California Press, 1969), pp. 86–117.

(VII, 49–50). In their innocence Adam and Eve are rather like two eager students who have been told they will pass their examinations if only they do not cheat. Error has not been made irresistibly alluring by this permissive guarantee since self-discipline remains rewarding and (at least in Eden) instinctive. Yet error is without final adverse consequence unless it leads, *as it clearly may*, to a basic violation of trust. Milton's paradise, then, is blessed with a conditional innocence, but it is not, because of this innocence, a place totally alien to fallen experience. Even in Eden Milton could not conceive of an effortless virtue, and because of this his account of man's fall continues to speak to the human condition. In no poem is the essential paradox of freedom more profoundly felt.

This dynamic paradise in which Adam and Eve may grow, "Improv'd by tract of time" (V, 498), but must also perform the "pleasant labor" (IV, 625) of restraint offers Milton the chance to show us something of ourselves in our first parents. He seems, in fact, to depict Adam and Eve by working back from the idea, articulated in *The Christian Doctrine*, that all sins were comprehended in the central act of disobedience:[5]

It comprehended at once distrust in the divine veracity, and a proportionate credulity in the assurance of Satan; unbelief; ingratitude; disobedience; gluttony; in the man excessive uxoriousness, in the woman a want of proper regard for her husband, in both an insensibility to the welfare of their offspring, and that offspring the whole human race; parricide, theft, invasion of the rights of others, sacrilege, deceit, presumption in aspiring to divine attributes, fraud in the means employed to attain the object, pride, and arrogance.

(C.E., XV, 181)

[5] See Bell, pp. 865–868.

If, Milton apparently reasons, this catalogue of error was comprehended in the single act of disobedience, one may fairly assume that all these sins were latent in unfallen man. Precisely this assumption has led to the frequent recriminations against Milton's God and to the conclusion that Adam and Eve were born sinners. It is clearly a disadvantage of Milton's scheme that intelligent readers can make this response (a response possible, of course, to all but the most heretical versions of the Christian God); however, Milton's emphasis here has its advantage in allowing him to make the drama of Eden forcefully relevant to his fallen audience. We can read in the record of our first parents' sojourn in paradise conflicts inherent in ourselves. What, in fact, we see dramatized in edenic man's "easy" exercises in self-restraint and verbalized in the instructive conversations between Raphael and Adam is what Milton elsewhere in *The Christian Doctrine* calls

The unwritten law . . . the law of nature given originally to Adam, and of which a certain remnant or imperfect illumination, still dwells in the hearts of all mankind; which, in the regenerate, under the influence of the Holy Spirit, is daily tending towards a renewal of its primitive brightness.

(C.E., XV, 101)

For Milton God's external prohibition was not Adam's only law; rather it was, to repeat, an outward sign of the inherent limitation which defines Adam's place in God's hierarchy—a place Adam is left free to maintain. Moreover, as this passage suggests, unfallen Adam's inner government anticipates the condition of regenerate man.[6]

[6] This point has been emphasized in Arthur E. Barker's valuable essay, "Structural and Doctrinal Pattern in Milton's Later Poems," *Essays in English Literature . . . Presented to A. S. P. Woodhouse,*

Clearly, in Milton's mind, seekers of the paradise within had much to learn from Adam whose control of a physical garden in *Paradise Lost* mirrors more than his own moral life; it mirrors theirs.

From this view of the continuity of God's ways with man, it might be inferred that the fall really matters very little. This, for Milton, is obviously not the case. In fact it is only by insisting on a sharp demarcation between fallen and unfallen states that difficulties arise in interpreting the so-called fortunate fall. If we are determined to consider paradise as a static, mindless holiday resort, it is hard to escape the feeling that sin has delivered man into a condition which more adequately challenges his native abilities, that man has lost very little and has, in fact, gained something. This is essentially Satan's argument, an argument most persuasively felt in the issue of knowledge.

Satan gains access to Eve by accusing God of an envious desire to keep man ignorant:

> *Why then was this forbid? Why but to awe,*
> *Why but to keep ye low and ignorant,*
> *His worshippers; he knows that in the day*
> *Ye Eat thereof, your Eyes that seem so clear,*
> *Yet are but dim, shall perfetly be then*

Millar MacLure and F. W. Watt, eds. (Toronto: Univ. of Toronto Press, 1946) pp. 169–194: "[The aim of the later poems was to induce] seventeenth-century Christian readers to realize the point of God's continuous ways by mimetic participation in the responses or failures of response of other men (or indeed of angels, since all creatures are involved) to their process, as it manifested itself in the circumstantially contrasting but essentially and developingly related conditions of other dispensations . . ." (pp. 173–174).

> *Op'n'd and clear'd, and ye shall be as Gods,*
> *Knowing both Good and Evil as they know.*
>   (IX, 703–709)

To Eve's literal and forgetful mind these persuasions make sense. God has indeed forbidden man the fruit of the tree of knowledge, and Milton seems deliberately intent on making this fact disturbing by allowing Adam and Eve to know, prior to disobedience, that God's prohibition involves specifically a tree "which tasted works knowledge of Good and Evil" (VII, 543). To supply Adam and Eve with this information, Milton has to alter his opinion in *The Christian Doctrine* that the tree "was called the tree of knowledge from the event" (C.E., XV, 115). This alteration is, I think, a matter of narrative strategy designed to link emphatically man's first disobedience with the exhilarating effort of inquiry which Milton so justly portrays as central to the activities of our newborn parents. Certainly it is perverse of Eve to suppose, at the point of her temptation, that God has elected to keep man ignorant of His ways. Adam and Eve know of God's goodness; they know of Satan's apostasy. They know also of their natural limitations, and it is this knowledge that Satan seeks to subvert.

For Milton intellectual aspiration lies at the heart of edenic experience. It is an aspiration God sanctions through the gift of reason and the ministry of Raphael who responds to Adam's hunger for knowledge and approves the appetite:

> *To ask or search I blame thee not, for Heav'n*
> *Is as the Book of God before thee set,*
> *Wherein to read his wond'rous Works . . . .*
>   (VIII, 66–68)

But as in all things human this appetite requires governance. In Raphael's pregnant metaphor which clearly anticipates the condition of fallen man,

> . . . *Knowledge is as food, and needs no less*
> *Her Temperance over Appetite, to know*
> *In measure what the mind may well contain,*
> *Oppresses else with Surfeit, and soon turns*
> *Wisdom to Folly, as Nourishment to Wind.*
>   (VII, 126–130)

Here Milton displays for us the symbolic aspect of the forbidden tree. To obey God in this crucial instance is to recognize that fundamental tenet of "the unwritten law," temperance, a tenet instructing men to keep their middle state, perfect yet limited. To disobey God's single external prohibition by plucking the fruit of knowledge constitutes in *Paradise Lost* an act of intemperance, a denial of place:

> *Man disobeying,*
> *Disloyal breaks his fealty, and sins*
> *Against the high Supremacy of Heav'n,*
> *Affecting God-head, and so losing all* . . . .
>   (III, 203–206)

In God's universe where all things are "Proportioned to each kind" (V, 479), man's aspiration to knowledge, if not accompanied by a sense of limitation, includes the danger of satanic overreaching, of an unwarranted questing for transcendence. God's threatening prediction of the fall in Book III is echoed in the actual temptation of man where the knowledge promised by Satan is equated directly with godhead—an equation the Devil seems almost to believe:

> *Hence I will excite thir minds*
> *With more desire to know, and to reject*
> *Envious commands, invented with design*
> *To keep them low whom Knowledge might exalt*
> *Equal with Gods . . . .*
>
> (IV, 522–527; see also IX, 703–709 quoted above)

Here, as Sherman Hawkins has aptly put it, is "a heresy invented by the Enemy."[7] Disobedience does not increase man's knowledge or his capacity for knowledge. Quite the contrary: the fall matters precisely because it plunges man into darkness. What man might be said to "gain" by disobedience is the knowledge of evil *in himself*, satanic knowledge which veils him from the understanding of God, the understanding which was, for Milton, the end of all proper intellectual inquiry. Milton's frequently cited statement from *Areopagitica* explains this consequence of the fall with perfect succinctness: "And perhaps this is that doom which *Adam* fell into of knowing good and evil, that is to say, of knowing good by evil" (C.E., IV, 310–311).[8] Adam, at the end of Milton's epic, may be offered a "paradise within . . . happier far" (XII, 587) than the paradise he has lost, but Milton nowhere suggests that this inward paradise can be more fortunate than what, for unfallen Adam, might have been, as he progressed unencumbered by the obscurity of his fallen nature toward an angelic state (V, 493–503).[9] In his early

[7] Sherman H. Hawkins, "Samson's Catharsis," *Milton Studies*, James D. Simmonds, ed., 2 (1970), 211. I am here indebted to Hawkins for more than the phrase.

[8] See also *The Christian Doctrine*, C.E., XV, 115.

[9] See John S. Diekhoff, *Milton's "Paradise Lost"* (New York: Columbia Univ. Press, 1946), pp. 130–131. Also see Lawrence A. Sasek, "The Drama of *Paradise Lost*, Books XI and XII," in Barker,

work Milton had held high hopes for the future of human society, but even in the more optimistic days of *Areopagitica* he never suggested that such hopes might include, on this side of the final Advent, a more intimate acquaintance with the truth of God's ways than would have been possible without the fall. His was, indeed, the opposite view:

> . . . the sad friends of truth, such as durst appear, imitating the careful search that Isis made for the mangled body of Osiris, went up and down gathering up limb by limb as they could find them. We have not yet found them all, Lords and Commons, nor ever shall do, till her master's second coming.
>
> (C.E., IV, 338)

The image of truth has been shattered by the fall. "To repair the ruins of our first parents" and "to know God aright"[10] Adam's seed must enter into burdensome conflict. The hard road to recovered paradise runs "Through all temptation" and must be travelled in "firm obedience fully tried" (*Paradise Regained*, I, 45).

Yet, as I have argued, conflict, temptation, and the necessity of obedience are not new to fallen man. They are also, in a less agonizing aspect, fundamental to prelapsarian experience. The search for truth in Eden, as in the fallen world, must proceed with due recognition of place. As Raphael tells Adam,

---

ed., *Milton: Modern Essays in Criticism*, pp. 345–355. Sasek points out that "Michael's tale of misery . . . contradict[s] any argument that the fall was fortunate . . . . Michael is merely saying [in describing the paradise within] that Adam will be happier with a good conscience outside Paradise than he would be with a bad conscience within Paradise." This opinion, I think, makes too little of the paradise within.

[10] *Of Education*, C.E., IV, 277.

> *God to remove his ways from human sense,*
> *Plac'd Heav'n from Earth so far, that earthly sight,*
> If it presume, *might err in things too high,*
> *And no advantage gain.*
>   (VIII, 119–122; my emphasis)

This warning against presumption, which is not, clearly, a denial of man's right of inquiry, is echoed by Michael who similarly instructs fallen Adam that beyond what God allows him to know it is "folly to aspire" (XII, 560). God's ways are constant, and because of this the fall in *Paradise Lost*, culminating as it does a *human* experience, serves as a warning for man and defines the conditions under which knowledge may be properly sought—subservience and obedience to the Deity.

II

Such a warning, while instructive to men in general, was of particular significance to John Milton in his assumption of a poetic ministry. Milton viewed man's primal experience in the quest for knowledge as inescapably relevant to his own intention of singing God's ways, and he chose to insist on this relevance in his epic by creating structured parallels between the poet's "advent'rous" exploration into the realm of truth and Adam's encounters with the various voices who speak for God. It is not, for example, an accident that within one hundred lines of the poet's request to his Muse for safe descent from the battlefields of Heaven to the "narrower bound" of the created world—"Descend from Heav'n *Urania*" (VII, 1) —we encounter Adam similarly asking Raphael to turn from his narration of an angelic action to the creation of man's own "visible Diurnal Sphere" (VII, 22):

> *Deign to descend now lower, and relate*
> *What may no less perhaps avail us known,*
> *How first began this Heav'n which we behold*
> *Distant so high, with moving Fires adorn'd*
> *Innumerable . . . .*
>
> (VII, 84–88)

Both Milton and Adam have been taxed by the strained metaphors of the angelic war, and their similar concerns here, as often in *Paradise Lost*, find similar utterance.

The import of this particular parallel involves the limitations of knowledge—limitations, shortly to be explained by Raphael (VIII, 119–122; quoted above), which obviously apply to the poet who is himself wary lest his own vision of heavenly events prove the unwarranted presumption of "An Earthly Guest" (VII, 13–14). In a similar but more general way Adam's subsequent reaction to Raphael's abridgment of astronomical speculation (VIII, 179–216) speaks again to the issue of the narrator's poetical flights beyond the reach of man's natural capacities. Here, while pat verbal parallels are lacking and the self-directedness of Milton's account is less obtrusive, a position centrally relevant to the poet's personal attitude toward knowledge in *Paradise Lost* receives its edenic statement:

> *. . . to know*
> *That which before us lies in daily life,*
> *Is the prime Wisdom; what is more, is fume,*
> *Or emptiness, or fond impertinence,*

> *And renders us in things that most concern*
> *Unpractic'd, unprepar'd, and still to seek.*
> *Therefore from this high pitch let us descend*
> *A lower flight, and speak of things at hand*
> *Useful . . . .*
>
> (VIII, 192–200)

While Adam is not, in these lines, rejecting what he has learned of Heaven, his criterion for the avoidance of fume is clearly nothing more complex than usefulness proportioned to "daily" existence, that existence which has sometimes been felt to bear the stamp of an oppressive domesticity. If this educational program is applied to Milton's practices in writing *Paradise Lost*, it may well seem that some of the poet's more esoteric flights—the satanic creation of cannon, for example, or the exact description of angelic intercourse—are extended beyond the limits of knowledge useful for such "daily life." Perhaps this humble measure of domestic utility is tailored to fit only a world of innocence. There is, no doubt, some truth in this estimate. Milton's paradise, for all its anticipations of the fallen world, is still paradise—a world uncluttered by the accretions of man's fallen history. Yet much that seems arcane is revealed to unfallen Adam, and Adam's summation here is emphatic enough to suggest a relevance for more than prelapsarian man, particularly since our parent's retreat from astronomical speculation concludes a discussion which few have claimed to be anything less than Milton's comment on one of the central scientific issues of his own time. A more adequate view of what might appear as a contradiction between Adam's "prime Wisdom" and the poet's encyclopedic epic resides, I think, in a proper understanding of what Milton considered essentially useful for "daily life"—his own or Adam's—and in a unified view of his moral intention in *Paradise Lost*.

This intention is, as the opening lines announce, to "assert Eternal Providence." All the rich complexity of Milton's epic is finally marshalled toward the assertion of Providence, and nothing, for Milton, was of more crucial importance for "daily life" than the continuing conviction of a providential God. His most personal tensions are resolved by this conviction: "So much the rather thou . . . / Shine inward" (III, 51–52); "All is, if I have grace to use it so, / As ever in my great task-Master's eye" (Sonnet VII); "who best / Bear his mild yoke, they serve him best" (Sonnet XIX). And it is finally "Providence" which guides our fallen parents eastward out of Eden. Only if *Paradise Lost* is read as a compendium of unrelated facts and speculations will the poet appear at times to have wandered into idle detail or fanciful guesswork. At their most abstruse and imaginative Milton's poetic flights can be justified not only by the belief in inspiration but by the ultimate concern to employ a poetic talent in the assertion of God's Providence. Even the war in Heaven, in all its lameness and grotesquery, remains functional in that it exists as a human symbol of God's power to direct the worst of events toward good. In his apologetic preface to the war, Raphael makes this point: the heavenly cataclysm, a subject beyond man's understanding and therefore debased in the telling, can be related in Eden only as a fiction, a shadow justified by the intention of revealing to man, for his own good, the eternal Providence of God.

The issue for Milton with respect to man's pursuit of knowledge finally does not so much involve *what* man may aspire to know as *how* and *to what ends* he seeks knowledge. Even for Adam the danger of "matters hid" resides not primarily in the subjects themselves but in the intellectual process which may lead man to pursue such subjects. "Wand'ring thoughts, and notions vain" are what he has come to fear, for "apt the Mind or Fancy is to rove / Uncheckt, and of her roving is not end" (VIII, 187–189). Some knowledge "Not of Earth only but of highest Heav'n" (VIII, 178) can and must be granted to Adam. What he is warned to guard against is not knowledge but the unchecked pursuit of knowledge. Such sheer intellectual speculation, such "studious thoughts abstruse" (VIII, 40) which do not ultimately seek to magnify God in man's understanding but evidence rather a self-inflating curiosity are what Raphael censures in Adam's questioning of the celestial machinery. Adam is free "to ask or search" (VIII, 66), but he must understand that God's secrets are not "to be scann'd by them who ought / Rather admire" (VIII, 74–75). Adam clearly grasps this:

> . . . wee not to explore the secrets ask
> Of his Eternal Empire, but the more
> To magnify his works, the more we know . . . .
> (VII, 95–97)

The necessity of this admiration is central to Milton's belief. His attitude toward scientific "fact," toward second causes, is at best indifferent; rather it is the consideration of nature with an eye to the first cause which, as Adam discovers, leads man closer to a proper understanding of God:

> *O favorable Spirit, propitious guest,*
> *Well hast thou taught the way that might direct*
> *Our knowledge, and the scale of Nature set*
> *From centre to circumference, whereon*
> *In contemplation of created things*
> *By steps we may ascend to God.*
>
> (V, 507–512)

This is a far cry from the new science.[11]

Thus for Milton, the pursuit of knowledge in Eden involves fundamentally a matter of intention: the proper end of curiosity is the glorification of God not man. Man is asked, in the midst of the exhilaration of an expanding consciousness, to rejoice in personal limitation, hierarchical inferiority, and infinite debt for all he surveys. He is asked to respond to an increasing awareness of his own powers with an increased reverence for powers not his own. In one form or another the difficulties and tensions inherent in this situation are familiar to everyone. At the heart of Milton's vision of Eden lies the painful realization that just such tensions—not their resolution—define the character of our lives. Milton's primal man is no cardboard archetype to be piously and mechanically acknowl-

---

[11] In a more elaborate cultural context Kester Svendsen has made a similar point: *Milton and Science* (Cambridge, Mass.: Harvard Univ. Press, 1946), pp. 237, 241: "the science in . . . [Milton's] works is mainly classical in origin, medieval in implication, literary in function . . . . The poems 'believe' in science the way they believe in classical mythology; the real truth is not in it except as it is analogue."

edged progenitor and pattern. As poetic seer Milton feels
Adam, new and old, within.

III

The limits of man's pursuit of knowledge are of course
partly dependent on the character of his natural intelligence. Milton's confidence in the power of man's intellectual faculties varied from the conservatism of the
antiprelatical tracts to the buoyant rationalism of *Areopagitica*, but nowhere did he suggest that the intellect's
proper governor, reason, when divorced from God's revelation, was anything but a feeble resource.[12] If at times
in his writings he is openly optimistic about man's
chances of knowing God aright, this optimism is measured by his sense of the abundance of God's favor. The
human need for divine assistance is, as I have been insisting, the essential statement of the prologues of *Paradise Lost*. It is a conviction repeated frequently throughout the poem, and, in particular, it is the lesson to be
learned from the first episodes in the history of man.
Without divine guidance, administered from without
rather than through man's rational faculties, Adam and
Eve would have wandered far down the path of error
without the help of Satan. The fact that God sends a
ministering angel, Raphael, to "advise . . . [unfallen man]
of his happy state" (V, 234) suggests man's need for
direct heavenly instruction. Newborn Adam himself
realizes that his visionary dream and subsequent con-
versation with the Creator are necessary supplements to

[12] For discussion of Milton's attitudes toward reason and revelation see Howard Schultz, *Milton and Forbidden Knowledge*, esp.
ch. III; Fish, ch. VI; and below, pp. 85–96.

his own self-discovery (VIII, 311–314), and newly created Eve similarly requires a warning voice to correct the
error of her natural impulses and reveal to her her proper
place. As Eve "With unexperienc't thought" (IV, 457)
bends down to view herself in the "Smooth Lake," the
covert allusion to the legend of Narcissus conveys with
remarkable aptness the point that absorption in the self
constitutes not only an error of misdirected affection but
also the mistake basic to all error—self-dependence. Eve's
natural understanding plays her false and will again.
Here she obeys the corrective voice of divine instruction
which curbs her impulse to "vain desire" by leading her
to "where no shadow stays / . . . [her] coming" (IV, 470–
471). Milton, in this episode, is repeating the lesson that
only obedience to the grace of God's guiding hand suffices
to reveal the illusory nature of self-love. This guidance is
soon to be ignored with tragic consequences.

The fall, to repeat, increases man's need for direct
manifestations of God's grace. Our first parents find their
"minds darkened." Adam frequently misconstrues his
vision of biblical history, the iniquities of which appear
at times "to [his] nature seeming meet" (XI, 604), and
without the assistance of Michael's interpretations, he
would clearly distort the purpose of what he sees. Finally
the fallen poet, echoing our first parent's prostrate hope
for heavenly favor (X, 1060–1104), gives periodic testimony by his prayers to a heavenly Muse that man's
natural faculties are, by themselves, unequal to the demands of this fallen world. As ever in his writings Milton
here maintains the primacy of revelation over "the weak
mightines of man's reasoning."[13] In *Paradise Lost* the

[13] *The Reason of Church Government*, C.E., III, 246.

poet's affinities with Adam and Eve involve centrally these limitations of reason, and because of this it will be useful to examine briefly reason's role in the fall of man.

Despite its limitations, reason in the upright man is first among man's natural gifts. On the day of the fall Adam explains the quality and function of reason to Eve and at the same time warns her of its deficiencies:

> *O Woman, best are all things as the will*
> *Of God ordain'd them, his creating hand*
> *Nothing imperfet or deficient left*
> *Of all that he Created, much less Man,*
> *Of aught that might his happy State secure,*
> *Secure from outward force; within himself*
> *The danger lies, yet lies within his power:*
> *Against his will he can receive no harm.*
> *But God left free the Will, for what obeys*
> *Reason, is free, and Reason he made right,*
> *But bid her well beware, and still erect,*
> *Lest by some fair appearing good surpris'd*
> *She dictate false, and misinform the Will*
> *To do what God expressly hath forbid.*
>
> (IX, 343–356)

In Adam's analysis reason appears as ruler of the will, but Adam also warns his wife that in reason lies the potential to "dictate false." While in Eve's fall, as is often said, passion triumphs over reason,[14] it is also true to say that here Eve's reason participates in its own unseating. Satan is successful in perverting reason in Eve to his own uses. Adam has told his spouse that

[14] See in particular Marjorie Hope Nicolson, "Milton and the Cabbala," *PQ*, 6 (1927), 17.

> . . . *Reason not impossibly may meet*
> *Some specious object by the Foe suborn'd*
> *And fall into deception unaware,*
> *Not keeping strictest watch*, as she was warn'd.
>
> (IX, 360–363; my emphasis)

Eve and her reason have been specially warned by God and by Adam, and it is precisely such warnings that Eve closets in a dark corner of her mind as, armed primarily with natural reason, she sets out to try what the Devil will do. Her departure from Adam's side is marked by Milton with a flood of references to pagan nature and to hapless pagan goddesses like Pomona and Proserpina (IX, 385–396)—references which emphasize the dependence of this "unsupported flower" on her natural faculties alone. Faced with the tempter, Eve is overcome by a manipulation and subversion of her natural reason through "some fair appearing good." Milton's presentation of this encounter is pointed: the serpent, appearing "As when of old some Orator renown'd / In Athens or free Rome, where Eloquence / Flourish'd, since mute, to some great cause addrest / Stood in himself collected" (IX, 670–673), delivers what seem to Eve "persuasive words, impregn'd / With Reason" (IX, 737–738). Eve's former boast, "Reason is our guide," echoes ironically when her rational faculties clearly assist in her decision to eat by providing her with the mechanisms of logic—mechanisms she employs in the service of sophistic rationalization:

> *For good unknown, sure is not had, or had*
> *And yet unknown, is as not had at all.*
> *In plain then, what forbids he but to know,*

> *Forbids us good, forbids us to be wise?*
> *Such prohibitions bind not.*
>   (IX, 756–760)

Never, for Milton, was man's gift of "discourse" worse employed.[15]

Natural reason, then, is not enough to prevent Eve's fall. Adam's case is similar. Unlike Eve his understanding is not so much subverted as it is ignored. Adam, the stronger vessel, is not able to convince himself sophistically of the rightness of wrong, but his passion for Eve overcomes his wisdom. His is a purer case of passion being given simple priority over reason in its "right" aspect, but in both cases the central point is the same: self-government based entirely on natural human faculties and oblivious to man's dependence on divine revelation is insufficient. Man, like the devils, may have been created "sufficient to have stood" (III, 99), but this sufficiency clearly includes the necessity of hearkening to God's warnings and commands. As Milton puts it in *The Christian Doctrine*, "No one . . . can have right thoughts of God, with nature or reason alone as his guide, independent of the word or message of God" (C.E., XIV, 31).

As I have already suggested, what is essentially denied by both our parents is degree—degree which requires of man an awareness of his middle state, "Magnanimous to correspond with Heaven / But grateful to acknowledge

---

[15] See Raphael's analysis of "Discursive" and "Intuitive" reason (V, 479–490). Northrop Frye's distinction between true reason and rationalization is clarifying here. In his explanation, Eve's reason is reduced by Satan's deceptive appeals to rationalization, the mechanical operation of the intellect which "enlist[s] reason in the service of passion" (p. 97).

whence his good / Descends" (VII, 511–513). Eve, ignoring "whence . . . [her] good / Descends" aspires to godhead; Adam, neglecting his magnanimity is overcome by a passion unworthy of his condition—what Raphael calls "the sense of touch" (VIII, 579). In his admiration for Eve, Adam sets aside what God has provided for him: a knowledge of the divine hierarchy. In choosing to eat the fruit, he resigns his "Manhood and the Place / Wherein God set [him]" (X, 148–149). He descends to an existential view of his condition in which "Her doing seem'd to justify the deed" (X, 142). Even Adam's initial response to the enormity of Eve's sin betrays him by its confusion of hierarchical values:

> *O fairest of Creation, last and best*
> *Of all God's Works, Creature in whom excell'd*
> *Whatever can to sight or thought be form'd*
> *Holy, divine, good, amiable or sweet!*
> (IX, 896–899)

Milton, surely, was aware of the apparent nobility of Adam's choice to share Eve's sin, just as he was aware of the human appeal of warlike heroism which is denigrated in the prologue to Book IX and consigned to Hell in Books I and II. His point is that God requires of man a perspective that reaches beyond himself toward his ultimate dependence on God. As many have said, Milton allows his audience a sympathetic response to Adam's uxorious choice in order to remind us all of our share in Adam's tragedy.

This is essentially the suggestion I have already made, and this is the reason I have been lingering over the circumstances of the fall: Milton uses these circumstances as a warning for fallen man in general and, in particular, as a warning for the fallen poet whose situation is consistently made to resemble aspects of our first parents' passage through Eden. To recall this situation, the blind poet, dwelling in darkness, is in search of visionary guidance which is centrally figured as light. Through the illumination of divine inspiration he seeks, in another metaphor, to "soar above th' *Aonian* Mount" with "no middle flight"; but, at the same time, his attitude toward these high aspirations remains uncertain. His historical situation or England's climate or his years may "damp . . . [his] intended wing / Deprest" (IX, 45–46). More threateningly, it appears that what he takes to be divine inspiration may "all be mine," in which case *Paradise Lost* becomes in fact a monument to vanity. The desire to understand the ways of Heaven, the blindness, the search for light, the yearning to soar are all recalled in the temptations of our first parents. Satan, boasting of his powers "not only to discern / Things in thir Causes, but to trace the ways / Of highest Agents" (IX, 681–683), promises Eve

> . . . *that in the day*
> *Ye Eat thereof, your Eyes that seem so clear*
> *Yet are but dim, shall perfetly be then*
> *Op'n'd and clear'd, and ye shall be as Gods . . . .*
>   (IX, 705–708)

Appearing as Eve's guide to greater knowledge, the serpent offers light, but it is "delusive Light" and not the divine illumination required by the poet to avoid the "wandering" fate of Bellerophon:

> *So glistered the dire Snake, and into fraud*
> *Led* Eve *our credulous Mother* . . . .
>
> (IX, 643–644)

>   . . . *as when a wand'ring Fire,*
> *Compact of unctuous vapor, which the Night*
> *Condenses, and the cold invirons round,*
> *Kindl'd through agitation to a Flame,*
> *Which oft, they say, some evil Spirit attends,*
> *Hovering and blazing with* delusive Light,
> *Misleads th' amaz'd Night-wanderer from his way*
> *To Bogs and Mires, and oft through Pond or Pool*
> *There swallow'd up and lost, from succor far.*
>
> (IX, 634–642; my emphasis)

This simile, which draws us from Eden into our fallen world, presents in the "amaz'd Night-wanderer" a future descendant of Eve, a descendant who bears an uncomfortable resemblance to the nocturnal poet who does not cease to "wander where the Muses haunt" and "Nightly" visits "Sion and the flowr'y Brooks beneath" (III, 27–32).

Following Satan's "delusive Light" Eve tastes the forbidden fruit and returns to Adam with a description of its effects which repeats the eye image so central to Milton's characterization of the poet:

> *This Tree is not as we are told, A Tree*
> *Of danger tasted, nor to evil unknown*
> *Op'ning the way, but of Divine effect*
> *To open Eyes, and make them Gods who taste* . . . .
>
> (IX, 863–866)

She has found herself new made:

> *. . . opener mine Eyes*
> *Dim erst, dilated Spirits, ampler Heart*
> *And growing up to Godhead . . . .*
> (IX, 875–877)

Adam replies to her account of increased clarity with words which recall the presumption of Milton's own "advent'rous Song": "Bold deed thou hast presum'd, advent'rous Eve" (IX, 921), but having followed Eve's example, he too discovers "op'n'd Eyes" (IX, 985) and "Divinity within . . . breeding wings / Wherewith to scorn the Earth" (IX, 1010–1011). Here Milton is again indirectly suggesting the dangers inherent in his own poetic flight, but he is also using the example of the fall finally to indicate the difference between the rebellion of our parents and his own *dependent* effort to sing God's ways. What Adam and Eve soon discover is that through disobedience only their carnal sight has been brightened; they have been correspondingly plunged into spiritual darkness:

> *. . . grosser sleep*
> *Bred of unkindly fumes, with conscious dreams*
> *Encumber'd, now had left them, up they rose*
> *As from unrest, and each the other viewing,*
> *Soon found thir Eyes how op'n'd, and thir minds*
> *How dark'n'd . . . .*
> (IX, 1049–1054; my emphasis)

Thus rising in sin, fallen Adam is compared to "the *Danite* strong / *Herculean Samson*" (IX, 1059–1060), and the associations which accrue to this allusion include

more than the immediately stated similarity between Eve
and "*Philistean Dalilah*"; the Samson whom Milton portrays "Eyeless in *Gaza*," but rousing himself to do God's
work, also lies in the background of this comparison, and
the association serves not only to project from the moment of man's greatest depth the promise of future grace;
it also suggests that physical obscurity, not carnally
"op'n'd Eyes," is to become an occasion for God's particular blessing. Such is the self-effacing darkness for
which guilty Adam yearns:

> *O might I here*
> *In solitude live savage, in some glade*
> *Obscur'd, where highest Woods impenetrable*
> *To Star or Sun-light, spread their umbrage broad,*
> *And brown as Evening: Cover me ye Pines*
> *Ye Cedars, with innumerable boughs*
> *Hide me, where I may never see them*
>   *[divine shapes] more.*
>
>   (IX, 1084–1090)

Light out of such darkness is the hope of the epic poet.

IV

The edenic comment on the poet's aspiration to knowledge is further amplified by Milton's frequent concern to
refer the daily activities of primal man to his own enterprise. These activities of Adam and Eve have been mem-
orably characterized by E. M. W. Tillyard as nothing if
not dull: "we feel that Milton, stranded in his own Paradise would very soon have eaten the apple on his own

responsibility and immediately justified the act in a polemical pamphlet."[16] I have already outlined the argument against this view of Milton's paradise, and I recall it—here in its liveliest expression—only to add one more objection: Milton would have found employment in Eden since, like Adam, he was a poet. The gardening Tillyard and others find so stultifying is repeatedly punctuated by song—song which like *Paradise Lost* glorifies God.[17] That this singing is to be compared to Milton's own song is apparent, initially, in the fact that the making of edenic poetry is unmistakably echoed by the poet's own manner of composition. The "various style" and "holy rapture," the "fit strains . . . Unmeditated," the "prompt eloquence" which flows from the lips of Adam and Eve "in Prose or numerous Verse" (V, 146–150) all recall Milton's picture of the poet who in mastering an "answerable style" is aided by "thoughts, that voluntary move / Harmonious numbers" (IX, 37–38) and a celestial patroness who "inspires / Easy my unpremeditated Verse" (IX, 23–24). Moreover, from Adam's lips not "ungraceful" and tongue not "ineloquent" even an angel—Raphael—does not scorn to learn "the ways of God with Man" (VIII, 218–226).

Milton's editors seldom neglect to point out that Adam's central exhortation of nature's abundant progeny to honor "the World's great Author" (V, 153–208) is

[16] *Milton*, p. 282. In *Studies in Milton* (London: Chatto and Windus, 1951), pp. 67–70, Tillyard repents of this opinion, but his reasons—(1) God intends paradise to be a temporary affair, and (2) Adam and Eve are meant to be on a honeymoon—are not, I think, altogether adequate.

[17] See Joseph H. Summers, *The Muse's Method* (Cambridge, Mass.: Harvard Univ. Press, 1962), p. 71.

based on Psalms, primarily on Psalm 148. Within the fiction of *Paradise Lost* this source serves as more than a reflection of the traditional cast of Milton's poem: here Adam, in his garden paradise, stands at the beginning as the forerunner of David, the hebraic pastoral singer. The address to natural objects which characterizes Adam's lovely hymn is typical generally of his utterances as the world's first singer. Finding himself newly created, Adam turns for an explanation of his being to the world about him and addresses it in what can be considered, if we recall the formula of Milton's own appeals to the powers of instruction, man's first poetic invocation:

> *Thou Sun, said I, fair Light,*
> *And thou enlight'n'd Earth, so fresh and gay*
> *Ye Hills and Dales, ye Rivers, Woods, and Plains*
> *And ye that live and move, fair Creatures, tell,*
> *Tell, if ye saw, how came I thus, how here?*
> (VIII, 273–277)

Man in his innocence here looks for the first time to powers external to himself; later, having eaten the forbidden fruit, Adam despondently recalls his past sympathy with unfallen nature:

> *O Woods, O Fountains, Hillocks, Dales and*
>   *Bow'rs.*
> *With other echo late I taught your Shades*
> *To answer, and resound far other Song.*
> (X, 860–862)

For Milton and his seventeenth-century reader not only the tradition of hebraic song but the tradition of pagan pastoral lay behind such evocations of man's harmony

with his natural setting. A specific instance of this is
the last line quoted here which echoes back through
Spenser to Virgil's first Eclogue; but more generally
Adam's mysterious rapport with nature would alone have
been enough to establish a pagan frame of reference. In
Paradise Lost Milton is more cautious than many poets
of the Renaissance in respect to the easy reading of sacred
truth in pagan story, but he certainly would not have been
reluctant to agree that all poets, in right or wrong divinity,
found their common ancestor in Adam. If Milton thinks
here of David as the hebraic descendant of Adam, then it
is natural to suppose he has Orpheus in mind as the proto-
type of pastoral singers whose comprehension of the
world had been deflected from the path of truth. The
pairing of Orpheus and David was commonplace in the
Renaissance. George Sandys, to pick a reliable example,
in englishing the *Metamorphoses* instructs his reader
that the music of Orpheus recalls the singing of "David
(who with his Harp subdues the evill Spirit which vexed
Saule), [and] introduced harmony into the Temple, as
suiting with that divine service";[18] or, in a more familiar
instance, Milton would have found these two pastoral
singers compared in Spenser:

> *Such as was Orpheus, that when strife was growen*
> *Amongst those famous ympes of Greece, did take*
> *His silver harpe in hand, and shortly friends them*
>   *make;*
> *Or such as that celestiall Psalmist was,*
> *That when the wicked feend his lord tormented,*

[18] George Sandys, *Ovid's Metamorphosis* . . . . (Oxford, 1632),
p. 356.

> *With heavenly notes, that did all other pas,*
> *The outrage of his furious fit relented.*[19]

Commentary on poetry from Augustine to Sidney and beyond commonly begins with Orpheus, the supposed author of the hymns bearing his name. Milton knew Orpheus as a singer of hymns;[20] only by deliberate omission could he have escaped relating Orpheus to his hebraic counterpart.

In *Paradise Lost* we find no such omission; rather we find Milton, with relaxed allusiveness, employing both Orpheus and David in his portrait of our first father. Adam, the ancestor of David, is also an orphic poet whose sympathetic addresses to nature recall the *"Thracian bard"* who, in the prologue to Book VII, is described singing "In *Rhodope*, where Woods and Rocks had Ears / To rapture" (VII, 35–37). This pagan aspect of Adam's rapport with his garden paradise is consonant with Milton's description of edenic nature in which the "Universal *Pan*" (IV, 266) of the orphic *Hymn to Pan* is discovered "knit with the *Graces* and the *Hours* in dance" leading "on th' Eternal Spring" (IV, 267–268).[21] In Milton's conception unfallen Adam possesses unique knowledge and power with respect to natural things. He and Eve keep "easy charge of all the Trees / In Paradise" (IV, 421–422); they are given "Dominion . . . / Over all other Creatures that possess / Earth, Air, and Sea" (IV,

[19] *The Faerie Queene*, IV, ii, 1–2.
[20] See C.E., XVIII, 294 and C.E., VII, 167.
[21] For illuminating discussion of the orphic lore surrounding the Graces and the Hours in the Renaissance see Edgar Wind, *Pagan Mysteries of the Renaissance*, rev. ed. (New York: Barnes and Noble, 1967), esp. his chapter on Botticelli's *Primavera*.

430–432); and Adam, echoing Genesis 2:19, tells Raphael
that when God's creatures passed before him "I named
them, as they pass'd, and understood / Thir Nature, with
such knowledge God endu'd / My sudden apprehension"
(VIII, 352–354).[22] Adam's wisdom and control of natural
things, his agency in harmonizing—almost like Pan himself—the variety of his earthly paradise, is underscored
by Milton's oblique allusion to Orpheus who, in the
Renaissance mind, had become particularly significant
for his power and knowledge in natural magic. Although
peculiar in some of his enthusiasms, Henry Reynolds presents an emphatic but representative statement of this
reading of Orpheus:

There is nothing of greater efficacy than the hymns of Orpheus in natural magic [i.e., "the exact and absolute knowledge of all natural things"], if the fitting musick, intention
of mind, and other circumstances which are knowne to the
wise, be considered and applyed. And again,—that they are
of no less power in natural magick or to the understanding
thereof than the Psalms of David are in the Caball . . . .[23]

That Milton was on civil terms with this aspect of orphic
lore seems apparent from his allusion to Orpheus in *Ad
Patrem* (52–55) and from his seventh prolusion where he
recalls with warm, if somewhat playful, approval that
"The very trees, and shrubs, and the entire forest tore

[22] Adam's naming of the animals was widely interpreted in
hexaemeral commentary as a sign of his profound natural wisdom.
See Evans, pp. 39–40, 94–95, 258–259.
[23] Henry Reynolds, "Mythomystes" in *Critical Essays of the
Seventeenth Century*, J. E. Spingarn, ed. (Oxford: The Clarendon
Press, 1908–1909), p. 166. Reynolds is translating and expounding
Pico.

away from their roots to run after the elegant music of Orpheus . . . . Rocks also respond with some docility to the sacred voice of the poets" (Hughes' translation, p. 629).

We can see, then, that Renaissance associations with the poet-magus, Orpheus, suggest his adaptability for Milton's purposes in describing Adam, the first poet of nature. It is also clear from a glance at the span of Milton's works that the Thracian bard is a recurring figure in his considerations of poetry and the fate of poets. Douglas Bush, observing Milton's preoccupation with Orpheus, has in fact found in this pagan figure a recurrent measure of Milton's attitudes toward his spiritual vocation:

Perhaps the most suggestive summary of . . . [Milton's] artistic and spiritual evolution is given in his allusions to Orpheus. The passage in *L'Allegro* partook of the unclouded lyricism of the whole (and that, to be sure, represented only one side of the serious young poet). Then, half a dozen years later, came the disenchanted questioning of the harsh lines in *Lycidas* on the death of the archetypal poet. Some thirty years later we have a partly similar antithesis between two allusions in the invocations of *Paradise Lost*.[24]

The two allusions to which Bush refers occur in the invocation to Book III where the poet in rising from Hell appropriately likens himself, contrastingly, to the pagan singer who likewise ventured the depths of Hades (III, 15–16) and in the prologue to Book VII where Milton recalls the Orpheus whose muse had proved ineffectual against

[24] Douglas Bush, *Mythology and the Renaissance Tradition in English Poetry*, rev. ed. (New York: W. W. Norton, 1963), p. 296.

> . . . *the barbarous dissonance*
> *Of* Bacchus *and his Revellers, the Race*
> *Of that wild Rout that tore the* Thracian *Bard*
> *In* Rhodope, *where Woods and Rocks had Ears*
> *To rapture, till the savage clamor drown'd*
> *Both Harp and Voice; nor could the Muse defend*
> *Her Son. So fail not thou, who thee implores:*
> *For thou art Heavn'ly, shee an empty dream.*
>   (VII, 32–39)

The poet of *Paradise Lost*, relying on his celestial patroness who by Book IX "deigns / Her nightly visitation
unimplored" (IX, 21–22), must trust that *his* nocturnal
Muse will not prove "an empty dream"; and his hope is
nurtured by the history of the first orphic singer, Adam,
who even in his state of sin is not dependent on Calliope
for protection: his ultimate fate is instead governed by
heavenly direction and heavenly mercy. Here, finally, is
the difference between Adam and Orpheus, a difference
underscored by yet another commonplace Renaissance
reading of the orphic myth. If Orpheus could be a decayed
image of the first Adam, so could he be seen as a mytho-
logical anticipation of the second Adam whose "evangelical music" moved the world to a true perception of
God's ways.[25] In comparing both the epic poet and Adam
to Orpheus, Milton, in a manner we shall find character-

---

[25] I refer here, as an instance, to Alexander Ross, *Mystagogus
Poeticus*, 6th ed. (London, 1675), p. 338: "Christ is the true *Orpheus*, who by the sweetness and force of his Evangelical musick
caused the Gentiles, who before were stocks and stones in knowledge, and no better than beasts in Religion, to follow after him:
It was he only who went down to hell to recover the Church his
Spouse, who had lost her self . . . ."

istic of him, looks toward the Son of God as the perfect exemplar for poets and for all men.

This final divergence of myth and truth can recall us to the crucial fact that while, for Milton, David and Orpheus were similar, they were not the same—a fact which suggests the initial relevance of Milton's comparison of the epic poet and the poet Adam: in relating Adam to *both* the hebraic and hellenic traditions of poetry, Milton is again commenting on his intense concern with the proper sources of poetic inspiration. David, in Milton's portrait of Adam, is clearly the ascendant figure, his psalm being the chief source of our parents' central hymn. This primacy of David over Orpheus corresponds, I would guess, to Milton's disposition with respect to his own poetic affinities. But the pagan sources of Milton's poetry are everywhere apparent in *Paradise Lost*, and by imbedding orphic impulses to song in Adam, Milton is also suggesting, as many others had suggested, that such impulses are not necessarily without God's sanction. Indeed, Adam's initial invocation of the wonders of creation (VIII, 273–277; quoted above) is both perfectly innocent and, because Adam has yet no direct knowledge of God, perfectly pagan. In effect Milton, who finally never denied the fundamental goodness of nature, is maintaining that the composition of *Paradise Lost* depends on a conjunction of natural impulses and the grace of God's direction. As C. A. Patrides has argued in his study of Christian tradition, Milton believed with St. Jerome that "Nature it selfe is in the last resolution of Grace, for God gave [us] that."[26]

---

[26] C. A. Patrides, *Milton and the Christian Tradition* (Oxford: The Clarendon Press, 1966), pp. 214–16.

In *Paradise Lost* Milton's explicit statement of his
effort to employ the complimentary and ultimately coinci-
dent resources of nature and grace occurs in the invocation to Book III:

> *Yet not the more*
> *Cease I to wander where the Muses haunt*
> *Clear Spring, or shady Grove, or Sunny Hill,*
> *Smit with the love of sacred Song; but chief*
> *Thee* Sion *and the flow'ry Brooks beneath*
> *That wash thy hallow'd feet, and warbling flow,*
> *Nightly I visit . . . .*
>
> (III, 26–32)

This magnificent passage seems to offer us, conceptually,
a clear distinction between poetry to be sought at the
haunts of the muses and the poetry which can come out
of Sion; but the uniform loveliness of the verse leaves us,
in the end, little to choose. The word *sacred* here seems
similarly to blur the distinction between nature and grace,
even as the distinction is blurred by Jerome "in the last
resolution." To call pagan poetry *sacred*—a word Milton
uses elsewhere to describe the chorus of angels (III, 369)
—is to underscore what Milton appears eager to suggest:
that such poetry is not forbidden fruit for the Christian
poet. Yet while Milton is bestowing a measure of sanctity
on pagan song, he is at the same time using the word
sacred and the line containing it to allude to Virgil's second Georgic—an allusion which emphasizes the distinctly
orphic nature of the muses' song. The Virgilian passage
Milton recalls is a direct appeal to the pagan muses to
reveal the secrets of nature:

> *Me vero primum dulces ante omnia Musae,*
> *quarum sacra fero ingenti percussus amore,*
> *accipiant caelique vias et sidera monstrent*
> *defectus solis varios lunaeque labores;*
> *unde tremor terris, quo vi maria lato tumescant*
> *obicibus ruptis rursusque in se ipsa residant,*
> *quid tantum Oceano properent se tinguere soles*
> *hiberni, vel quae tardis mora noctibus obstet.*[27]

By first compounding Christian and pagan meanings in the phrase "sacred Song," and then partially unfolding this ambiguity with "but chief / Thee *Sion*," Milton finally suggests something like a hierarchy in his sources of inspiration, but a hierarchy which does not insist, as a more rigorous Puritan might have it, that pagan light and Christian truth are totally incompatible. Like nature and grace, the one can be comprehended in the other; both can be infolded in the concept, *sacred*.[28] For Milton the poetry and wisdom of the pagan past were not lightly discarded, yet at the same time the pagan muses, as re-

---

[27] Virgil, *Eclogues, Georgics, Aeneid, I-VI* (Loeb Classical Library), *Georgics*, II, 475–482. The lines may be translated: "First, above all, may the sweet muses whose sacred things I bear (smitten with great love) truly receive me and show me the ways of heaven, the stars, the sun's many failings and the labors of the moon; whence come the tremors of the earth, the force that makes the deep seas swell, break their bounds and subside into themselves; why the winter suns hasten so to dip themselves in the ocean or what delays detain the lingering night."

[28] See A. S. P. Woodhouse, "Pattern in *Paradise Lost*," *UTQ*, 22 (1952–1953), 113: "In utilizing it [the distinction between nature and grace] Milton never fails to accord full recognition to the beauty and worth of the natural order while maintaining always its subordination to the higher order."

vealed by the example of the unfortunate Orpheus, were not ultimately dependable. Poetry loosed from a contact with divine inspiration could be turned to the uses of Satan. This again is the lesson of Eden.

V

The poet Adam is more than a singer of hymns; he is also a poet of love whose aubade to Eve relates him, as do his hymns, to the tradition of hebraic poetry:

> *Awake*
> *My fairest, my espous'd, my latest found,*
> *Heav'n's last best gift, my ever new delight,*
> *Awake, the morning shines, and the fresh field*
> *Calls us; we lose the prime, to mark how spring*
> *Our tended Plants, how blows the Citron Grove,*
> *What drops the Myrrh, and what the balmy Reed,*
> *How Nature paints her colors, how the Bee*
> *Sits on the Bloom extracting liquid sweet.*
> (V, 17–25)

These verses, which recall The Song of Solomon, 2:10–13, are set in direct opposition to the satanic serenade of Eve's dream:

> *Why sleep'st thou Eve? now is the pleasant time,*
> *The cool, the silent, save where silence yields*
> *To the night-warbling Bird, that now awake*
> *Tunes sweetest his love-labor'd song; now reigns*
> *Full Orb'd the Moon, and with more pleasing light*
> *Shadowy sets off the face of things; in vain,*
> *If none regard; Heav'n wakes with all his eyes,*
> *Whom to behold but thee, Nature's desire,*

> *In whose sight all things joy, with ravishment*
> *Attracted by thy beauty still to gaze.*
>
> (V, 38–47)

In passages separated by only a dozen lines, Satan plays "Il Penseroso" to Adam's "L'Allegro." The most obvious contrast here is the one Howard Schultz observes between Adam, the bridegroom, and Satan the "Cavalier seducer" or "vulgar amorist" who sings the "serenate" which Milton, elsewhere in his burst of enthusiastic praise for married love, labels that "which the starv'd Lover sings / To his proud fair, best quitted with disdain" (IV, 769–770).[29] This contrast, moreover, relates to the distinction Milton has been making between divine poetry and the poetry of purely natural impulse, between David and Orpheus, between grace and nature. Here, in the hands of Satan, the order of nature, now obscured from grace, can be perverted; the "Full Orb'd Moon" becomes "more pleasing light," and Eve is falsely elevated to become the wonder of all the eyes of Heaven. But as so often in Milton, the contrast is not simple. In this case a satanic lure—"the night-warbling Bird, that now awake / Tunes sweetest"—distinctly recalls the epic poet himself who "as the wakeful Bird / Sings darkling, and in shadiest Covert hid / Tunes her nocturnal Note" (III, 38–40). A. S. P. Woodhouse comments a little irritably,

Again coming to focus in the image of the nightingale, there is the recognition that night may be the hour of poetic inspiration; and this, I suppose, might be construed as one of

---

[29] Howard Schultz, "Satan's Serenade," *PQ*, 17 (1948), 17–26. See also Harold E. Toliver, "Complicity of the Voice in Paradise Lost," *MLQ*, 25 (1964), 153–170.

those paradoxes dear to the new criticism; for what it suggests is that darkness, the enemy, may turn out to be a friend in disguise.[30]

Woodhouse is reluctant to sound like a new critic, but the characteristic tensions of *Paradise Lost* force him to recognize Milton's, not his colleagues', attraction to paradox. Here, audaciously, Milton again fits the Devil and the poet with the same image, and the paradox inherent in this is intended, I think, to force the reader to seek an explanation. As I have argued in the preceding chapter, Milton's willingness to expose the potential for sin in his own epic wayfaring is a part of his reiterated emphasis on the complexities of good and evil and on the dangers involved in his attempt to combine the lights of nature, classical education, and divine inspiration. Without the superior efficacy of his heavenly muse, he here suggests, the "wakeful Bird" of the prologues may become a satanic night-warbler.

In respect to poetry, then, the argument of Milton's Eden asserts the superiority of divine song, insists on the dangers characteristic of the purely orphic utterance, but also leaves room for the poet to employ his natural talent and to consider monuments of the pagan past. The deficiencies of this pagan culture are most harshly assessed by Milton in the Son's notorious answer to Satan in *Paradise Regained* where Sion's songs are exalted at the expense of the arts of Greece (IV, 334–352). Among admirers of Milton's humanism, the Son's sweeping criticism of Hellenism—matched in strength, no doubt, to its

[30] Woodhouse, p. 113; Woodhouse is commenting on the prologue to Book III, not on the lines referring to Satan which echo this prologue. The point, however, is essentially the same.

demonic respondent—has frequently been a source of concern; but even in repelling the profane enticements of Satan Milton does not finally deny all wisdom to pagan authors who may still express "moral virtue ... / By light of Nature, not in all quite lost" (IV, 351–352). Milton can still "wander where the Muses haunt." What the Son emphasizes is that this light is dim and capable of being eclipsed by a satanic shadow. We have already seen Milton's wariness of demonic influences; for him, as we shall see, the possibility of direct satanic inspiration had already been realized in Eden.

VI

In his poem of dedication, Marvell confessed to initial fears that given his subject Milton might "ruin ... / The sacred Truths to Fable and old Song" or perplex "the things he would explain / And what was easy ... render vain." This concern was not only for the violation of sacred truth: Marvell also had fears for the poet himself, and here he was of a mind with Milton who begins his second invocation by asking,

> *Hail holy Light, offspring of Heav'n first born,*
> *Or of th' Eternal Coeternal beam*
> *May I express thee unblam'd? since God is*
> *Light . . . .*

> (III, 1–3)

He may express holy light only by submitting his creative powers to it, to the heavenly muse, to Urania, "the meaning not the Name" (VII, 5), and to his celestial patroness, all of whom are manifestations of God's condescension. If Milton had not believed literally in his own divine in-

spiration, if his invocations were nothing more than to-
kens to epic convention, *Paradise Lost*, in its own terms,
would be nothing short of blasphemy. If divine inspiration is received, however, Milton can, without impious
presumption, hope to "tell / Of things invisible to mortal
sight" (III, 54–55).[31] Evidence that Milton was confident
of God's assistance in some great undertaking is not, of
course, hard to find. Particularly in his early expressions
of commitment to a poetic vocation—in *The Reason of
Church Government*, for example, or in *Ad Patrem*—he
sounds unequivocally assured of God's particular favor.
But clearly even the regenerate cannot presume on God's
benevolences, and in his epic Milton is concerned much
more than in his earlier utterances to make clear that
while he trusts in God, he does not, of his own merit,
command what God alone must choose to bestow, that
indeed the writing of this poem remains a precarious attempt, an "advent'rous Song" full of dangers for the
singer. In Book IX, as we have seen, the poet concludes
his personal prologues with an admission that the efficacy
of his inspiration continues to be in doubt. His "higher

[31] See Howard Schultz's important discussion of Milton's attitude
toward religious enthusiasm in *Milton and Forbidden Knowledge*,
pp. 148–156. Schultz is right to insist that Milton never abandoned
his allegiance to the scriptures and to reason. However, I think
Schultz's concern with Milton's doctrinal affinities yields a dis-
torted view of the invocations in *Paradise Lost* (Schultz feels they
"hardly deserve attention" as evidence of Milton's attitude toward
the Spirit). In his epic Milton was not just concerned with achiev-
ing the "answerable style" Schultz calls the essential concern of
these passages. There is more of the inspired prophet in Milton
than this. To "see and tell / Of things invisible to mortal sight"
requires vision as well as eloquence.

Argument" will be "sufficient of itself to raise / That name [heroic]"

> . . . *unless an age too late or cold*
> *Climate, or Years damp my intended wing*
> *Deprest; and much they may, if all be mine,*
> *Not Hers who brings it nightly to my Ear.*
>   (IX, 42–47)

The words "if all be mine" imply the possibility of self-deception on the part of the poet; perhaps all is not "Hers"; perhaps the poet, without knowing it, is falsely inspired or self-inflated. Yet in the next line there is no equivocation in the phrase, "brings it nightly to my Ear." Milton asserts the muse's visitations at the same time that he admits she may be absent or at least ineffectual. If there is illogic here, it is the distinctive illogic of a Christian faith which demands simultaneously a trust in God and a fear of Him. For Milton, while he may possess a consciousness of present grace,[32] this consciousness derives in him primarily from faith not knowledge. Knowledge of God's ways with man is, as *Paradise Lost* argues, no insignificant matter with Milton. But Milton cannot know, ultimately, how God views his labors; finally he must depend on faith—a faith which averts spiritual pride through the humility displayed in an unwavering recognition of the need for grace and in constant sensitivity to mankind's capacity for error. A particular danger of error for Milton as a poet lies in vision, vision which may not come from heaven but may come nonetheless—as it does to Eve—without solicitation or warning.

[32] See *The Christian Doctrine*, C.E., XVI, 64–98.

Eve's dream, the work of Satan, is, despite its origins, an inspired vision:

> *Squat like a Toad, close at the ear of* Eve;
> *Assaying by his Devilish art to reach*
> *The Organs of her Fancy, and with them forge*
> *Illusions as he list, Phantasms and Dreams,*
> *Or if, inspiring venom, he might taint*
> *Th' animal spirits* . . . .
>
> (IV, 800–805)

Satan here is literally "inspiring" Eve, breathing in venom to "taint" her intellectual faculties until they produce "Vain hopes, vain aims, inordinate thoughts, / Blown up with high conceits ingend'ring pride" (IV, 808–809).[33] That Milton could have written these lines without thinking of his own hopes and aims seems unlikely if one recalls his insistence that as epic poet his own inspiration is brought "nightly to . . . [his] Ear." Milton's muse, the muse he hopes for and trusts in, appears as

> *. . . my Celestial Patroness, who deigns*
> *Her nightly visitation unimplor'd*
> *And dictates to me slumbring, or inspires*
> *Easy my unpremeditated Verse* . . . .
>
> (IX, 21–24)

---

[33] The serpent is similarly inspired:

> *. . . in at his Mouth*
> *The Devil enter'd, and his brutal sense,*
> *In heart or head, possessing soon inspir'd*
> *With act intelligential* . . . .
>
> (IX, 187–190)

These circumstances of inspiration have been described earlier in Book VII:

> *In darkness and with dangers compast round,*
> *And solitude; yet not alone, while thou*
> *Visit'st my slumbers Nightly, or when Morn*
> *Purples the East . . . .*
>
> (VII, 27–30)

Even the postures of Eve's dream recall the soaring poet of the prologues:

> *Forthwith up to the Clouds*
> *With him I flew, and underneath beheld*
> *The Earth outstretcht immense, a prospect wide*
> *And various: wond'ring at my flight and change*
> *To this high exaltation . . . .*
>
> (V, 86–90)

Unfallen Adam and Eve are able to recognize, at least partially, the nature of Satan's nocturnal attempt. The danger of delusion for the fallen poet is clearly greater. By echoing in Eve's dream his own visionary experience Milton projects his recognition of this danger and asserts faith as his ultimate defense against the Devil.

The poet's nightly visions are an extension of the light in darkness paradox Milton constructs using the fact of his own blindness:

> *Thus with the year*
> *Seasons return, but not to me returns*
> *Day, or the sweet approach of Ev'n or Morn,*
> *Or sight of vernal bloom, or Summer's Rose,*
> *Or flocks, or herds, or human face divine;*
> *But cloud instead, and ever-during dark*

> *Surrounds me, from the cheerful ways of men*
> *Cut off, and for the Book of knowledge fair*
> *Presented with a Universal blanc*
> *Of Nature's works to me expung'd and ras'd*
> *And wisdom at one entrance quite shut out.*
> *So much the rather thou Celestial Light*
> *Shine inward, and the mind through all her powers*
> *Irradiate, there plant eyes, all mist from thence*
> *Purge and disperse, that I may see and tell*
> *Of things invisible to mortal sight.*
>
> (III, 40–55)

These lines expand the buried suggestions of physical blindness which appear in the first invocation ("what in me is dark / Illumine" and the allusion to "Siloa's Brook" where Christ healed the blind man), and they serve to strengthen the impression of human weakness out of which Milton asserts the necessity of God's grace. This process in which the blunting of the physical senses is accompanied by a correspondent sharpening of spiritual insight is repeated often in the narrative proper of *Paradise Lost*, primarily in connection with our first parents. Adam's initial view of paradise, like Eve's disturbing vision, comes in a dream; his view of Eve's birth occurs "as in a trance" with "eyes . . . closed, but op'n . . . the Cell / Of Fancy my internal sight" (VIII, 460–463); and fallen Adam's final Pisgah view of humanity's future similarly transcends the waking senses in a manner which echoes the poet's visionary triumph over blindness:[34]

[34] On the eye in *Paradise Lost* see in particular A. B. Chambers, "Wisdom at One Entrance Quite Shut Out: *Paradise Lost*, III, 1–55," in Barker's collection of essays, pp. 218–225. For an illuminating discussion of sacred blindness see Wind, ch. IV.

> *. . . but to nobler sights*
> *Michael from Adam's eyes the Film remov'd*
> *Which that false Fruit that promis'd clearer sight*
> *Had bred; then purg'd with Euphrasy and Rue*
> *The visual Nerve, for he had much to see;*
> *And from the Well of Life three drops instill'd.*
> *So deep the power of these Ingredients pierc'd,*
> *Ev'n to the inmost seat of mental sight,*
> *That Adam now enforc't to close his eyes,*
> *Sunk down and all his Spirits became intranst:*
> *But him the gentle Angel by the hand*
> *Soon rais'd, and his attention thus recall'd.*
> (XI, 411–422)

Blindness in *Paradise Lost* emerges gradually as a correlative for the middle state of man. It serves as a metaphor which even God employs:

> *. . . I will clear thir senses dark,*
> *What may suffice, and soft'n stony hearts*
> *To pray . . . .*
> *This is my long sufferance and my day of grace*
> *They who neglect and scorn, shall never taste:*
> *But hard he hard'n'd, blind he blinded more . . . .*
> (III, 188–190; 198–200)

A measure of Milton's personal involvement in his poem is the fact that not just spiritual darkness but physical sightlessness becomes the characteristic occasion of God's grace. Elsewhere, goaded into self-defense by the attacks of the *Regii Sanguinis Clamor* which had proclaimed his loss of sight to be the punishment of God, Milton enthusiastically embraced the blessing of blindness:

There is, as the apostle has remarked, a way to strength through weakness. Let me then be the most feeble creature alive, as long as that feebleness serves to invigorate the energies of my rational and immortal spirit; as long as in that obscurity, in which I am enveloped, the light of the divine presence more clearly shines; then, in proportion as I am blind, I shall more clearly see. O! that I may thus be perfected by feebleness, and irradiated by obscurity! And, indeed, in my blindness, I enjoy in no inconsiderable degree the favor of the Deity, who regards me with more tenderness and compassion in proportion as I am able to behold nothing but himself.[35]

"Strength through weakness," now less flamboyantly but steadily asserted, is the promise of *Paradise Lost.*

What Milton shows us in Eden are two kinds of inward, visionary experience: Eve's satanic dream and Adam's trancelike visitations of divinity. Because there is no precedent for Eve's dream in hexaemeral tradition, its inclusion in *Paradise Lost* seems carefully calculated and has usually been viewed as a dramatic foreshadowing of the fall. It may be this,[36] but in addition, I think, it serves as a comment on the precarious nature of the dream-visions enjoyed not only by the poet but also by Adam. This comment is focused most sharply in Milton's explicit contrasting of Adam's first vision of the world and the lush poetic masterpiece created for our first mother by Satan.[37] Adam relates that, having innocently considered the source of his own creation,

[35] *The Second Defense of the English People*, C.E., VIII, 73.

[36] For an argument that Eve's dream does not foreshadow the fall see Stanley E. Fish, "Discovery as Form in *Paradise Lost*," *New Essays on "Paradise Lost*," Thomas Kranidas, ed. (Berkeley: Univ. of California Press, 1969), pp. 1–14.

[37] This contrast has been recently remarked by Frye, pp. 74–76.

> Pensive I sat me down; there gentle sleep
> First found me, and with soft oppression seiz'd
> My drowsed sense, untroubl'd, though I thought
> I then was passing to my former state
> Insensible, and forthwith to dissolve:
> When suddenly stood at my Head a dream,
> Whose inward apparition gently mov'd
> My fancy to believe I yet had being,
> And liv'd: One came, methought, of shape Divine,
> And said, thy Mansion wants thee, Adam, rise,
> First Man, of Men innumerable ordain'd
> First Father, call'd by thee I come thy Guide
> To the Garden of bliss, thy seat prepar'd.
>
> (VIII, 287–299)

Certain correspondences between this passage and Eve's later dream, such as the appearance of a figure at the sleeper's head, are merely the conventional trappings of literary dream lore,[38] but other parallels are clearly more pointed. Both dreamers are unsure of the identity of their visionary guides. To Adam "One came, methought of shape Divine"; Eve first thinks the voice which calls her is Adam but later discerns "One shap'd and wing'd like one of those from Heav'n" (V, 55). In both cases the dreamer is caught in a world of phantoms in which appearances created free from the curbs of reason through the "Organs of . . . Fancy" or the "animal spirits," provide the primary criteria of choice. To Eve the "Tree / Of interdicted knowledge" (V, 51–52) seems fair. Recalling

[38] On the relation of literary dream conventions to Milton see William B. Hunter, "Eve's Daemonic Dream," *ELH*, 13 (1946), 255–264.

God's command she is at first "chill'd" by "damp horror" (V, 65) at the false angel's "vent'rous" eating of the
fruit, but "the pleasant savory smell / So quick'n'd appetite that I, methought / Could not but taste" (V, 84–
86). Similarly Adam is moved by "Each Tree / Load'n
with fairest Fruit, that hung to the Eye / Tempting," trees
which stir in him "sudden appetite / To pluck and eat"
(VIII, 306–309). By insisting on the similarities between
the dreams of Adam and Eve, Milton seems concerned to
show us that the difference between the two inspired
visions is not so much one of quality as one of source.
In Eve's case appearances are a sham. Adam is, quite
simply, more fortunate; he awakes and finds "Before mine
Eyes all real, as the dream had lively shadow'd" (VIII,
310–311). Adam's dream-guide has been heavenly; Eve,
at the point of her highest "exaltation," discovers "sud-
denly / My Guide was gone" (V, 90–91). These words
resonate in *Paradise Lost*; they sound the extreme peril
of Eve's uncomprehending discovery. Man needs proper
guidance from above. He needs a Raphael, a Michael, a
"Safe Guide" (XI, 371), a "Celestial Guide" (XI, 785), a
"Heav'nly Instructor" (XI, 872), and "Enlightener of . . .
darkness" (XII, 271), *or* a "Celestial Patroness" to administer the revelation crucial to the maintenance of his
middle state.[39]

Adam, of course, is not deceived by what in Eve's
dream contradicts his knowledge of God. Neither, for
Milton, was fallen man, armed with the scriptures and
right reason a mere pawn in a cosmic game played by God
and the Devil. But in Eden false vision clearly represents
a threat which must be faced, a threat which becomes

[39] Eve mistakenly calls the fatal tree, "Best guide" (IX, 808).

more insidious for fallen man whose powers of perception
have been blurred by sin. Man's response to vision, as to
all things, can be no passive thing.[40] Adam, realizing evil
may come into the mind of God or man, is anything but
a blind enthusiast. Vision must be tested; it must be consonant with right reason, and it must conform to the dic-
tates of prior revelation. Finally, however, it can only
be affirmed by faith that God will provide "Light after
light" (III, 196) sufficient to these tests. At this point of
faith man's reason and knowledge cease, paradoxically,
to be distinctly his own. As man comes through faith to
participate in the divine will, the voice of God and his
ministers, transcending the merely human, are in the end
believed. Unfallen Adam awakes from his dream and confirms "all real," but his human capacity is not enough:

> *Here had new begun*
> *My wand'ring had not hee who was my Guide*
> *Up hither, from among the Trees appear'd*
> *Presence Divine. Rejoicing, but with awe,*
> *In adoration at his feet I fell*
> *Submiss . . . .*
>
> (VIII, 311–316)

Similarly, the purged eye of fallen Adam does not create
in him an intuitive perception of even visionary truth. As
he ascends "in the Visions of God" (XI, 377), he still
needs the word of Michael to correct the error of what
appears "to [his] Nature seeming meet" (XI, 604). Milton's comparison of two kinds of vision in Eden is

[40] Milton's attitude toward scriptural revelation is, for example,
similar. "Those written records pure" (XII, 513) require rational
consideration as well as the guidance of the Spirit for proper
understanding.

intended to suggest the dangers of false or miscon-
strued revelation—dangers which the inspired poet faces
"Nightly, or when Morn / Purples the East." The poet,
in full command both of his reason and his knowledge
of God's ways, must still, having done his part, trust that
his guide who appears "like one . . . from Heav'n" is what
she seems. Milton is not here surrendering his lifelong
advocacy of reason and, as some have suspected, with-
drawing into pietism; rather he is repeating his rational
estimation of man's ultimate and continuing debt to God.

VII

I have been arguing that the lesson of the fall for primal man is essentially the lesson of place—place defined
by obedience and the recognition of natural limitation.
Yet Adam, as we have seen, need not have fallen to learn
this lesson. Before the fall, as after, he is aware of his
proper position in God's universal order, as his cautiously
deferential interrogation of Raphael reveals:

>   *. . . sudden mind arose*
> *In* Adam, *not to let th' occasion pass*
> *Given him by this great Conference to know*
> *Of things above this World, and of thir being*
> *Who dwell in Heav'n, whose excellence he saw*
> *Transcend his own so far, whose radiant forms*
> *Divine effulgence, whose high Power so far*
> *Exceeded human, and his wary speech*
> *Thus to th' Empyreal Minister he fram'd.*
>
>   *Inhabitant with God, now know I well*
> *Thy favor, in this honor done to Man,*

> *Under whose lowly roof thou has voutsaf't*
> *To enter . . . .*
>
> (V, 452–464)

Not only Adam's curiosity, but his posture here could serve as a model for the aspiring poet's attempt "to know / Of things above this World," but Adam forgets the obeisance owed to his superiors and must learn again. His reeducation begins with his sense of sin's consequence and ends with his vision of the future of his race. With Michael's assistance this vision becomes an instruction in the proper conduct of life, a revelation for man of "the sum / Of wisdom" (XII, 575–576). That the scope of the vision's relevance includes, among others, the Christian poet is emphasized at the outset in that the central doubt Michael labors to allay, while it is spoken by Adam, is also the precise question *Paradise Lost* addresses:

> *. . . why has thou added*
> *The sense of endless woes? inexplicable*
> *Thy Justice seems . . . .*
>
> (X, 753–755)

Michael's vindication of God's justice and his explanation of man's duties in the world encompass, in brief scope, vast areas which in being ordered primarily by the course of biblical history, have seemed to some an artless addendum—in the often quoted opinion of C. S. Lewis, an "untransmuted lump."[41] Yet while Books XI and XII

---

[41] *A Preface to 'Paradise Lost'* (London: Oxford Univ. Press, 1942), p. 129.

—particularly XII—seem at times little more than biblical paraphrase it is certainly not true that the material they contain is "untransmuted." Michael's history bears the stamp of attitudes and problems central to Milton's particular concerns within *Paradise Lost* and without: it is vivid in its descriptions of feminine allurement and "Ill-mated Marriage" (XI, 684); it is expansive in its attack on tyranny and its praise of true liberty; it repeatedly portrays solitary men of virtue like Noah and Enoch who persevere alone in decadent societies, societies "cool'd in zeal" and practicing "how to live secure" (XI, 801–802); and it reinforces one of the most important concerns of *Paradise Lost* in its embittered rebuke of false heroism:

> For in those days Might only shall be admir'd
> And Valor and Heroic Virtue call'd;
> To overcome in Battle, and subdue
> Nations, and bring home spoils with infinite
> Man-slaughter, shall be held the highest pitch
> Of human Glory, and for Glory done
> Of triumph, to be styl'd great Conquerors,
> Patrons of Mankind, Gods, and Sons of Gods,
> Destroyers rightlier call'd and Plagues of Men.
> (XI, 689–697)

This rejection of the heroic standard of the past bears directly on the concerns of the Christian poet who, as Milton maintains, should not be "sedulous by Nature to indite / Wars, hitherto the only Argument / Heroic deem'd" (IX, 27–29). Among Milton's most audacious departures from the tradition of former epic was his conception in *Paradise Lost* of a heroic poem in which arms would be no essential measure of human valor but would instead be the glory and the bane of Hell itself.

In this attitude toward the heroic, Milton's poetic concerns are, as so frequently in *Paradise Lost*, simply an extension of his general sense of the proprieties of living in a fallen world. For Milton, the artist and his art must conform to universally applicable Christian standards, and in the vision which closes *Paradise Lost*, Michael's description of "the tents / Of wickedness" makes this point directly for the last time. Within these tents are displayed arts which must surely be seen as the demonic antitheses of Milton's own art:

> . . . *studious they appear*
> *Of the arts that polish Life, Inventors rare,*
> *Unmindful of thir Maker, though his Spirit*
> *Taught them, but they his gifts acknowledg'd*
>   *none.*
>
> (XI, 609–612)

These "Inventors rare, / Unmindful of thir Maker" represent, for Milton, precisely what the Christian poet is not. Mindfulness of God's gifts is the keynote of Milton's prologues, and this mindfulness is the ultimate burden of Michael's message for man:

> *He ended; and thus* Adam *last repli'd* . . . .
> *Greatly instructed I shall hence depart*
> *Greatly in peace of thought, and have my fill*
> *Of knowledge, what this Vessel can contain;*
> *Beyond which was my folly to aspire.*
> *Henceforth I learn, that to obey is best,*
> *And love with fear the only God, to walk*

> *As ever in his presence, ever to observe*
> *His providence, and on him sole depend,*
> *Merciful over all his works, with good*
> *Still overcoming evil, and by small*
> *Accomplishing great things, by things deem'd*
>   *weak*
> *Subverting worldly strong, and worldly wise*
> *By simply meek; that suffering for Truth's sake*
> *Is fortitude to highest victory.*
> *And to the faithful Death the Gate of Life . . . .*
>
>   (XII, 552–571)

Aspiration limited by a sense of place; with respect to God, love with fear, obedience, dependence, observation of His providence; with respect to man, great things accomplished by small, weak overcoming strong, and truth the end of suffering. When Michael adds "Deeds to thy knowledge answerable" (XII, 582), a description of the epic poet is nearly complete. It should surprise no one that Milton's conception of the ideal Christian poet coincides with his conception of the ideal Christian. But in *Paradise Lost*, as we have seen, such simplicity of conception yields a complex interplay between poet and narrative in which the poet's characters continually remind us in their words and actions of the problem of decorum faced by the soaring poet. In the sins of Satan and of our first parents we become aware of the subtle snares that can entrap the aspiring mind, and prompted by repeated analogies between poet and character we begin to understand the force of Milton's concern with the dangers inherent in his own aspirations. In singing *Paradise Lost* the poet seems repeatedly to be considering his own case, to be strengthening himself, even, from his adventure in epic narrative. Michael's instruction summarizes all that the poet has labored not to forget, and one final aspect of this lesson recalls what is certainly the crucial element of Milton's posture as poet. Adam learns in his conduct of life to be "Taught . . . by his example whom I now / Acknowledge my Redeemer ever blest" (XII, 572–573). The poet's adherence to this tenet will be the subject of my concluding chapter.

3: The Angelic Narrators

I

WITHIN THE narrative of *Paradise Lost*, the only explicit statements of poetic theory belong to Raphael who assumes, as does Michael, the role of epic narrator. For more than a quarter of the length of Milton's poem the voice of the epic singer is angelic. This is largely a matter of narrative expediency, but not entirely so. By substituting angelic voices for his own, Milton also suggests that, in a way peculiar only to a divinely inspired poet, his own singing of God's ways follows angelic precedent. Like Raphael the poet attempts to describe "what surmounts the reach / Of human sense" (V, 571–572), and like Michael his intent is to justify the ways of God to man.[1] Milton, as we have seen, finds demonic and edenic

[1] Even Uriel is given a brief chance to sing, like the poet and like Raphael, the world's creation. In *Milton's Epic Voice* (Cambridge, Mass.: Harvard Univ. Press, 1963) Anne Ferry suggests that the angels "speak a different language" (p. 70) from the poet. While I agree that the angelic voices have their distinctive qualities (see below, pp. 111–142) it is not my impression that their narratives are as stylistically unique as Mrs. Ferry suggests. For example her contention that "Raphael's similes reveal the nature of his vision and also of Adam's . . . and so must draw on comparisons from within his [Adam's] experience" (p. 71) seems only partly true.

activity crucially relevant to his situation as aspiring poet. Similarly, but in a more positive way, he looks to his conception of angelic ministry for a pattern of the Christian poet, a pattern more perfect than Adam and antithetical to the example of Satan. In *Paradise Lost* Raphael and Michael reveal to us by precept and example something of what, for Milton, were the limitations and the range of Christian poetry. In turn what Raphael and Michael teach us of Milton's preoccupation with a Christian decorum can help us, I will be arguing, to understand some of the less impressive sections of the epic—namely, the war in Heaven and Adam's final revelation.

Let me begin by suggesting some of the ways in which Milton allusively associates the poet with God's angelic agents. As ministers of God's effluence the angels are frequently described in terms of Milton's central metaphor for the knowledge the Almighty condescends to bestow on men—the traditional metaphor of light. The poet, as we have seen, "In darkness and with dangers compast round" (VII, 27), hopes to be sustained by divine inspiration which is figured as the "sovran vital Lamp" (III, 22) of holy Light. This metaphorical description relates centrally to God's general pronouncement that "Light after light" (III, 96) will be given to those who hear "My Umpire *Conscience*" (III, 195). Adam and Eve hear briefly God's umpire and are assisted in their attempt to be illuminated in the knowledge of God's ways by divine guidance administered frequently by heavenly messengers

---

Some of the very similes to which Mrs. Ferry refers—"timorous" flocks (VI, 857), flights of birds (V, 73–74)—derive from classical epic and therefore are directed beyond Adam's experience to the literary experiences of the poet and his reader.

who are called, appropriately and conventionally, "Sons
of Light" (V, 160; XI, 80). These angelic "Sons of Light"
are, of course, themselves dependent on the source of all
illumination, God who "is Light, / And never but in unapproached Light / Dwelt from Eternity" (III, 3–5). In
this dependence on God's effluence they resemble mankind—Adam, Eve, and particularly the poet who is not
only a recipient of holy Light but also, like the angels, an
agent of divine illumination. Conceptually, there is nothing particularly unique in Milton's scheme here, but in
his hands the metaphor of light makes itself felt profoundly and complexly as a mode through which God's
creatures experience His beneficence.

The poem's first angelic son of Light is Uriel, "Regent
of the Sun" (III, 690),

> . . . one of the sev'n
> Who in God's presence, nearest to his Throne
> Stand ready at command, and are his Eyes
> That run through all Heav'ns or down to th'
> Earth
> Bear his swift errands over moist and dry,
> O'er Sea and Land . . . .
>
> (III, 648–653)

Milton spares nothing to link this "Interpreter" (III, 657)
of God with light: Uriel's name, which Milton was the
first to match with the regency of the sun, translates from
the Hebrew as "fire of God" or "light of God" or perhaps
"God is my light";[2] the angel is "The same whom *John*

[2] For Milton's originality with respect to Uriel see Robert H.
West, *Milton and the Angels* (Athens, Ga.: Univ. of Georgia Press,
1955), p. 208. For discussions of Uriel's name see Hughes' note to

saw also in the Sun" (III, 623); in Book IV, it will be recalled, his ministry between Heaven and Earth virtually
metamorphoses him into a ray of light, "Gliding through
the Eve / On a Sun-beam, swift as a shooting Star" (IV,
555–556); and, as Davis Harding has observed, Milton
allusively links Uriel, crowned by a "golden tiar" "Of
beaming sunny rays" (III, 625), to Ovid's Sun-god of the
Phaeton myth.[3] Milton is obviously laboring here to surround this first of God's interpreters with an elaborate
complex of allusion and description which serves to
ground firmly the metaphorical conjunction of heavenly
ministry with light—a conjunction which suggests a fundamental link between poet and angel. Uriel makes his
initial appearance in Book III, the invocation to which
offers us Milton's most overt association of his own ministry with the light of God. Within the narrative of *Paradise Lost*, Uriel introduces a series of brilliant figures
who, like the poet Milton, transmit divine illumination
and reveal to minds less blessed "The Works of God"
(III, 695).

As interpreters of the Almighty, the angels and the
poet share, in different degrees, the difficulty of express-
ing the immensity and inscrutability of God and his
works. The poet's frequent expressions of concern for his
limitations in relating the infinite in finite terms are
echoed by the angels. When Uriel, for example, recalls
his duties and limitations before singing the creation to

III, 622 and Grant McColley, *"Paradise Lost": An Account of Its
Growth and Major Origins* . . . . (Chicago: Packard, 1940), p. 137.

[3] Davis P. Harding, *Milton and the Renaissance Ovid* (Urbana:
Univ. of Illinois Press, 1946), p. 92.

a disguised Satan, he speaks also for the narrator of
Paradise Lost:

> *. . . wonderful indeed are all his works,*
> *Pleasant to know, and worthiest to be all*
> *Had in remembrance always with delight;*
> *But what created mind can comprehend*
> *Thir number, or the wisdom infinite*
> *That brought them forth, but hid thir causes deep.*
>   (III, 702–707)

Uriel's description of the infinitude and mystery of God's
works which "no created mind can comprehend" must
surely weigh upon Milton when, through Raphael in
Book VII, he approaches his own song of the creation.
The sun-bright angel's testimony figures significantly in
the accumulating evidence for the intimidating immensity of the poet's epic undertaking.

Milton's second angelic minister is Raphael who, like
Uriel, is drawn in terms of the epic's major symbolic pat-
tern, light against darkness. When the sun has reached
its zenith, Raphael arrives in Eden like "another Morn /
Ris'n on mid-noon" (V, 310–311). Descending from
Heaven,

> *. . . he seems*
> *A* Phoenix, *gaz'd by all, as that sole Bird*
> *When to enshrine his reliques in the Sun's*
> *Bright Temple, to* Egyptian Thebes *he flies.*
>   (V, 271–274)

This allusion, if we follow its implications, is complex; it
serves in several ways to place Raphael within the poem's
total view of God's providence, and in so doing it helps

establish a kinship between the angel and the poet. The phoenix metaphor is, first, a part of a continued contrast between Raphael and Satan which, beginning with a comparison of their soaring flights into paradise (see V, 267–270 and III, 562–566) and their subsequent earthly walks through the "spicy" gardens of Eden (compare V, 291–299 with IV, 159–163), ends with a direct opposition in which the Devil and Raphael are twice recalled in conflict over "the Spouse / Of Tobit's Son" (IV, 169–170; see V, 221–223)—a conflict in which the spicy odors appropriate to the phoenix nest ("Myrrh, / . . . Cassia, Nard, and Balm" [V, 292–293])[4] are altered for Satan, to "the fishy fume, / That drove him . . . / . . . with a vengeance" (IV, 168–170).

This devil-angel polarity is further underscored by Milton's contrasting of Raphael as phoenix with Satan who halts his winged descent into paradise perched upon the tree of life "like a Cormorant" (IV, 196). Raphael's

---

[4] See Ovid, *Metamorphoses*, II (The Loeb Classical Library), XV, 395–401:

> haec [phoenica] ubi quinque suae conplevit saecula vitae
> ilicet in ramis tremulaeque cacumine palmae
> unguibus et puro nidum sibi construit ore,
> quo simul ac casias et nardi lenis aristas
> quassque cum fulva substravit cinnama murra,
> se super inponit finitque in odoribus aevum.

> [This bird, forsooth, when it has completed five centuries of life, builds for itself a nest in the topmost branches of a waving palm-tree, using his talons and his clean beak; and when he has covered this over with cassia-bark and light spikes of nard, broken cinnamon and yellow myrrha, he takes his place upon it and so ends his life amidst the odours.
>
>   (Loeb translation)]

phoenix-like ministry ultimately suggests, through the common Christian reading of the phoenix myth, the example of immortal Christ; in contrast, Satan, the infernal minister, is transformed here into a deadly fisher—of men. For Milton, the personal relevance of this reiterated polarity between angel and devil is suggested by what we have seen of the poet's negative comparison of himself to Satan. Here, in phoenix-like Raphael, is an explicit positive model for Christian ministry to replace the rejected demonic pattern.

But the phoenix allusion serves more directly than this to characterize Raphael as a heavenly exemplar of the poet: the imagery of flight with which Milton describes Raphael's phoenix-like visitation may serve to recall the soaring poet of the prologues (I, 14; III, 13; VII, 3–4; IX, 45–46); moreover, the aspect of the phoenix myth wherein the eternal bird cyclically returns to the shrine of light similarly recalls the poet who, in the invocation to Book III, has revisited holy light for a rebirth of visionary vitality. Elsewhere Milton employs the same myth to describe the rekindling of blinded Samson's vigor:

> . . . *[Samson] though blind of sight*
> *Despis'd and thought extinguish't quite,*
> *With inward eyes illuminated*
> *His fiery virtue rous'd*
> *From under ashes into sudden flame. . . .*
> *Like that self-begott'n bird*
> *In the Arabian woods embost . . .*
> *From out her ashy womb now teem'd,*
> *Revives, reflourishes, then vigorous most*
> *When most unactive deem'd . . . .*
> 　　　　　(*Samson Agonistes,* 1687–1705)

This passage helps to suggest the personal implications of the phoenix myth for the blind poet. The phoenix served Milton as an emblem for renewed strength, rebirth through light, the same process through which inspiration is experienced by the visionary singer whose own "quencht... Orbs" (III, 25) are rekindled inwardly by celestial Light:

> *So much the rather thou Celestial Light*
> *Shine inward, and the mind through all her*
> *   powers*
> *Irradiate, there plant eyes, all mist from thence*
> *Purge and disperse, that I may see and tell*
> *Of things invisible to mortal sight.*
>
> (III, 51–55)

Such multiple associations are in part possible because in the story of the phoenix Milton's light symbolism is given significant shape, the shape of providence—light out of darkness: "The world shall burn, and from her ashes spring / New Heaven and Earth wherein the just shall dwell" (III, 334–335).

The comparison of Raphael to the phoenix serves, then, to associate the poet with his angelic substitute who, not unlike Uriel, is concerned to express his limitations in the face of a demanding poetic subject:

> *... how [shall I] last unfold*
> *The secrets of another world, perhaps*
> *Not lawful to reveal?*
>
> (V, 568–570)

Such angelic reticence, as we shall see, is central to Milton's concern in creating a heavenly voice which will speak for himself in matters of poetic decorum.

Milton's last important son of Light is Michael. Like Raphael, he brings illumination to Eden, but befitting his sterner purpose he is surrounded by a more ominous brilliance. "Flaming Warriors" accompany him, and a fiery sword. He descends in a cloud of "radiant white" (XI, 206), but "Darkness ere Day's mid-course" (XI, 204) shadows his coming. This "blazing Cloud" (XI, 229) betokens a visitor not sociable but "solemn and sublime" (XI, 236); yet at the same time Michael's brightness links him symbolically with the other bearers of God's word to men. As God's agent, Michael's ministrations to fallen man are in several ways different from Raphael's amiable discussions with innocent Adam, and one of the most obvious differences is that half of Michael's message is delivered as vision, not narration. The poet, in imitating the ministering angels, does not follow Michael in this; he cannot presume, directly at least, to make visionaries of his readers. In administering Adam's vision of "the world destroyed" (XII, 3), Michael, the "Enlight'ner of . . . [Adam's] darkness" (XII, 271), is more like the poet's muse than like the poet himself, but when the burden of his message shifts to the "world restor'd" (XII, 3), Michael then becomes, like the narrator of *Paradise Lost*, a prophetic singer to whom God has granted special illumination:

> . . . *reveal*
> *To* Adam *what shall come in future days,*
> *As I shall thee enlighten . . . .*
> (XI, 113–115)

The reason for this shift from vision to narration may at first seem odd, arbitrary, or crudely transitional. But

Michael gives a justification for the change which is worth taking seriously because it relates, I think, to the value of divine poetry as Milton viewed it:

> *Thus thou hast seen one World begin and end;*
> *And Man as from a second stock proceed.*
> *Much thou hast yet to see, but I perceive*
> *Thy mortal sight to fail; objects divine*
> *Must needs impair and weary human sense:*
> *Henceforth what is to come I will relate,*
> *Thou therefore give due audience, and attend.*
>
> (XII, 6–12)

This is an estimate of fallen man's capacity for vision, vision which Milton identified as a burden even to the ancient prophets.[5] It is also a rationale for *Paradise Lost*, for a ministering theodicy which attempts to accommodate to the "mortal sight" of men the intense glare of holy Light.

II

The differences between Michael and Raphael are many and have been frequently noted. Not only does Michael add vision to the modes of angelic communication with man, his narrative style differs radically from the style of Raphael's two major poems, the war in Heaven and the song of creation. These differences, representing, as they do, variations in Milton's own epic style, are worth examining for what they tell us about Milton's

---

[5] See *The Reason of Church Government*, C.E., IV, 230–231. Eve's dreams are clearly not as strenuous as Adam's visions: "Her also I with gentle Dreams have calm'd / Portending good" (XII, 595–596).

conception of a decorum fitted to the precarious relation between the Christian poet and his subject.

Raphael has been called by Arthur Barker "the poet of the past merely," the poet who "operates through Dame Memory and her angelic daughters." By contrast Michael, in Barker's view, "is sent to reveal to Adam what shall come in the future, as God enlightens his angelic mind in terms appropriate to Adam's response to expulsion from Paradise and its implications. He is the Miltonic poet accommodating the truths of Christian experience to fallen man . . . ."[6] Suggestive as this distinction is, it can easily be construed to mean that somehow Michael's poetic mode constitutes a retrospective criticism of the epic's more flamboyant voices—of Raphael, for one, or the poet who sings of Hell.[7] I have been arguing, of course, that Milton viewed his poem as an adventure; it was, indeed, an adventure in which his own poetic virtuosity represented a primary danger. But while Milton in *Paradise Lost* clearly views his quest for an answerable style as precarious, he does not, I think, waver in his attitude toward the proprieties of his style as the poem progresses; he does not stumble toward a final "Miltonic" decorum. Even in the final prologue where he finds wars

[6] Arthur E. Barker, "Structural and Doctrinal Pattern in Milton's Later Poems," *Essays in English Literature . . .* , Miller MacLure and F. W. Watt, eds. (Toronto: Univ. of Toronto Press, 1964), pp. 187–188.

[7] Harold E. Toliver offers an interpretation along these lines in his valuable article, "Complicity of the Voice in *Paradise Lost*," *MLQ*, 25 (1964), 153–170. While Toliver and I differ in our sense of Milton's progress through *Paradise Lost*, his argument which views the epic voice as a participant in the poem's tonal movement anticipates mine in several important ways.

and the trappings of former epic insufficient *argument* for his purpose, his intention is not to look back over the course of what he has done and repudiate his borrowings from the heroic tradition. He need not reject or even apologize for Hell or the war in Heaven because he has repeatedly attempted to use heroic materials and methods within the limitations of his own constant sense of what is decorously suited to Christian poetry. From the initial invocation onward Milton is keenly sensitive to the problems of decorum posed by *Paradise Lost*, and his method of dealing with these problems displays not instability but variety and invention.

This variety is suggested by another of Barker's contrasts: while Michael is the more conventionally Christian poet, Raphael is "the 'Orphic' poet of prelapsarian nature; and his two poems represent the prelapsarian naturalistic Orphicism of which the remnants and as it were a reflection remain in all pagan Orphic poets . . . and in pagan myths."[8] If one views Raphael's song as existing prior to Milton's sense of literary tradition, Barker's description tells us something very useful about the sociable angel's poetic resources. However, if one is to call Michael a Christian poet, the question of a tradition begins to enter into the contrast between the two angelic ministers and serves to shift the basis of description. From Milton's vantage point as a seventeenth-century poet, the poetic modes of Raphael and Michael are neither purely Christian nor purely "Orphic," and it is this vantage point, I think, which tells us the most about Milton's attitude toward his poem.

[8] Barker, p. 188.

As any reader can readily verify, Raphael's "prelapsarian" utterances are grounded in biblical materials and Michael's Christian history is not untouched by Milton's debt to the pagan classics.[9] To be sure, the ratio between pagan and Christian borrowings shifts radically from Raphael's Homeric epic to Michael's biblical redaction, but since Milton's characteristic style is a humanistic fusion of pagan and Christian materials it might, in fact, be more proper to call Raphael the Miltonic poet rather than Michael whose narrative presents a more homogeneous aspect. Throughout *Paradise Lost* Milton maintains a synthesis of biblical and classical materials and the variations in emphasis he gives to these sources suggest, I think, not a groping for *the* proper decorum but an attempt to maintain a decorum requisite to his changing subject matter. No constant poetic mode could answer to the range of Milton's narrative. In *Paradise Lost* the relation between poet, reader, and subject alters drastically as the poem's action moves from Hell to Heaven to Earth, and Milton displays daring and ingenuity in attempting to maintain a decorum shaped to these alterations.

I wish to consider in some detail two instances of Milton's matching of matter and manner, Raphael's story of

[9] See Davis P. Harding, *The Club of Hercules* (Urbana: Univ. of Illinois Press, 1962), p. 68; and Lawrence A. Sasek, "The Drama of *Paradise Lost*, Books XI and XII," in Barker's collection of essays, pp. 343–344. Michael's instruction to Adam structurally echoes the hilltop vision offered to Aeneas by his father in the sixth book of the *Aeneid*. The visions Michael administers recall other instances of epic prophecy by drawing some of their scenic detail from the shields of Achilles (*Iliad*, XVIII, 478–608) and Aeneas (*Aeneid*, VIII, 626–728).

the heavenly war and Michael's presentation of biblical history. These narratives, which have offered embarrassments for Milton's apologists and opportunities for his denigrators, represent opposite issues with respect to decorum and can therefore serve to place in broad perspective Milton's conception of the Christian poet's difficulty in fashioning a style which could answer to the multiple demands of a cosmic view of providence.

III

Earth was within Milton's own "Diurnal Sphere"; Hell could be abused; but with the holy mysteries of Heaven desecration was, for the poet, an immediate danger. The war in Heaven, for which biblical authority was scant and expository comment was vexed,[10] offered Milton an extreme problem of decorum, a problem which would seem to have demanded a display of humility equal to the poet's hierarchical inferiority before the heavenly hosts. However, the common attitude toward Milton's bold use of homerics in Raphael's account of the war belies such an estimate of Milton's concerns. Here Milton is apparently willing to burden a slender strand of the hexaemeral tradition with the ponderous weight of epic machinery. According to generations of readers including Addison and Johnson, in this place where he should have been most wary of soiling Heaven with the mundane trappings of epic tradition, Milton shut his eyes to decorum. Even those who, like Newton, have admired the war's heroic grandeur are often forced by their sense of propriety into

[10] See C. A. Patrides, *Milton and the Christian Tradition* (Oxford: The Clarendon Press, 1966), p. 94.

apologies: "our author seems to have been betrayed into
. . . excess, in great measure, by his love and admiration
of Homer."[11] Johnson, arguing less charitably that an
"inconvenience of Milton's design is that it requires the
description of what cannot be described,"[12] turns what
for Newton was a localized flaw into a general criticism
of Books V and VI: "The confusion of spirit and matter
which pervades the whole narration . . . fills it with incongruity."[13] Both critics are sensitive to what Wayne
Shumaker, speaking for many in our century, has called
"the unsuitability of the metaphor to the semantic burden."[14] Shumaker, citing numerous instances of the "inconsistencies and self-contradictions" which result from
Milton's mismatching of an angelic subject and a style
derived primarily from those who sang arms, concludes
that the Homeric metaphor "is the wrong metaphor for
Milton's purpose. Elsewhere *Paradise Lost* is almost in-
vulnerable to any criticism except that which refuses to
grant the epic's preassumptions. In the War Milton undercuts his own ground, presumably because of a half-
bored acceptance of epic tradition."[15] It would seem,
however, that precisely because Milton here so openly
"undercuts his own ground" the conclusion that he was
nodding, that he was insensitive to incongruities which
readers from the eighteenth century to the twentieth

[11] Thomas Newton, ed., *Paradise Lost: A Poem in Twelve Books*
(London, 1749), n. to VI, 568.

[12] Samuel Johnson, *Works* (London, 1806), IX, 152.

[13] Johnson, IX, 153.

[14] Wayne Shumaker, *Unpremeditated Verse: Feeling and Perception in "Paradise Lost"* (Princeton: Princeton Univ. Press, 1967),
p. 119.

[15] Shumaker, p. 126.

have strongly felt, is untenable. Surely Milton goes out of his way in the prologue to Book IX to find "Battles feign'd ... / ... Races and Games / Or tilting Furniture" (IX, 31–34) material essentially inferior to his own epic argument. Such materials would seem at best suited to the bombastic world of Hell. Moreover, Milton's conception of Christian heroism plainly emerges as the antithesis of the warlike valor celebrated by earlier epic poets. Milton could not, I think, have forgotten matters so essential when he turned to describe a heavenly war, but if these attitudes were his, why, one wonders, did he allow his angels to adopt traditional heroic postures?

Arnold Stein, the war's most able defender, has provided an answer to this question by arguing with tact and sense that the incongruity between matter and manner is not Milton's error but his intention. Stein's thesis, briefly stated and shorn of its many valuable insights, is that the Homeric heaviness of the war is intended to deflate Satan's forces and that the clanking machinations of the rebel host not only provoke the ironic laughter of the Deity but are also intended to amuse the fit reader. Of the hurling of mountains, for example, Stein writes, "surely it is naive to think Milton straining for grandeur in this passage."[16] Such an observation gives Milton no more than his due. Stein's argument, however, is open to attack on several fronts. I cannot agree with those who simply reject the notion that something like mock heroic could find its way into an heroic poem, but it is, I think, fair to object that the mood of Books V and VI, despite all the punning and posturing, does not provoke much

[16] Arnold Stein, *Answerable Style: Essays on "Paradise Lost"* (Minneapolis: Univ. of Minnesota Press, 1953), p. 24.

laughter. A flying mountain comes off badly as a custard pie. A more serious objection involves the fact that the excessively strained heroics Stein describes ridicule fallen and unfallen angel alike, and despite Stein's admission that this is the case,[17] it is hard to agree that for a Christian, the mocking of God's faithful angels, for whatever reason, constitutes anything more than a failure of taste.[18] This problem is basic to any reading of Books V and VI, sympathetic or otherwise. Johnson was among the first to be disturbed by the similar treatment afforded both armies, and his comment can be used to define the issue:

. . . in the battle when . . . ["The vulgar inhabitants of Pandaemonium"] were overwhelmed by mountains their armour hurt them, "crushed in upon their substance, now grown gross by sinning." This likewise happened to be the uncorrupted angels, who were overthrown "the sooner for their arms, for unarmed they might easily as spirits have evaded by contraction or remove" . . . if they could have escaped without their armour, they might have escaped from it and left only the empty cover to be battered.[19]

The vision of Satan's forces ridiculously battering "the empty cover" is not, perhaps, inappropriate to Book VI, but the uncorrupted angels are not let off so easily. They are instead made to seem nearly as foolish as the satanic army by remaining needlessly encumbered. The Homeric cast of Raphael's narrative traps both armies, but surely God's forces have not "gross by sinning grown" (VI,

[17] Stein, p. 23.

[18] The sacred joke was not uncommon among writers of the Renaissance, but to my knowledge sacred mystery was seldom the butt of such drollery.

[19] Johnson, IX, 153.

661). That the materiality explicitly associated with sin should hamper the good angels is a blatant inconsistency which is all the more troubling for its being forced upon the reader rather than ignored.[20] Such deliberate awkwardness seems intended, as Stein suggests, to emphasize some kind of incongruity, but if the purpose of Milton's mismatching of style and subject is to ridicule Satan's "vain attempt," the similar mocking of the faithful angels remains unexplained.

Stanley Fish, while endorsing Stein's basic thesis, has pointed to this weakness: "Clearly, the difficulty of regarding the War in Heaven as mock heroic is that the heroics of the good angels are also mocked."[21] Fish avoids this difficulty by arguing that Milton's reason for placing the good angels in ridiculous postures is that he wishes to use them as examples of what his reader must learn: to serve God ungrudgingly in absurd and futile situations.[22] Patience and faith are certainly lessons to be learned from the war in Heaven, but it does seem to me that such lessons need not be purchased at the price of ridicule—a high price judging from the centuries of adverse reaction to Milton's weighty Homerics. If we can

---

[20] The two passages in question occur within seventy lines of each other (VI, 595–600; VI, 656–661).

[21] Stanley E. Fish, *Surprised by Sin* (New York: St. Martin's Press, 1967), p. 180.

[22] Fish, pp. 180–207. Joseph H. Summers, in his sympathetic reading of the war (*The Muse's Method* [Cambridge, Mass.: Harvard Univ. Press, 1962]), offers a similar explanation. He also suggests that "the comic . . . [is] only one of the perspectives here" (p. 122). I agree with this. In here emphasizing the comic and the issue of decorum, I by no means wish to deny that, particularly from a theological perspective, what happens in Books V and VI is crucial.

agree with Stein that Milton intended his Homeric metaphor to appear grotesque, there remains at least one more
way to understand this intent. What I wish to argue is
that we have here not mock heroic in which epic formulas
of action and language serve bombastically to sink an inadequate subject but, so to speak, mock*ed* heroic in
which poetic manner is intentionally depreciated by its
inability to answer adequately to the demands of a heavenly subject. Such a deliberate display of inadequacy on
the poet's part may at first appear simply self-defeating,
and I cannot argue for its ultimate success. However, that
Milton was not trying to defeat his own undertaking need
hardly be argued. From the poem's inception he had
found himself in an ambiguous position with respect to
his precursors in epic poetry. As a Christian humanist
with Puritan affinities he both admired and disapproved
of the tradition in which he found himself writing, and
in pursuing the course of his poem he now, with something like a war to describe, had arrived at a crucial
juncture with respect to this tradition.[23] His choices
were unequivocal: he must now reject the tradition out
of hand as unsuited to his subject or, in keeping with
his practice up until this point, embrace the tradition
and reshape it in some radical way. He made the latter
choice, grudgingly I think. He adopted the Homeric
mode, yet at the same time he was concerned to display
his awareness that his subject was beyond the reach of

[23] The war could not be avoided. It represented to Milton's mind
the archetypal instance of the victory of good over evil. As William B. Hunter, Jr., has shown ("Milton on the Exaltation of the
Son: The War in Heaven in *Paradise Lost,*" *ELH*, 36 [1969], 215–
231) the war comprehends the defeat of Satan before time, in time,
and at the end of time.

the traditional heroic style. For the renovator of traditional epic the only decorous style was now a faltering one. Let us look at the evidence for this estimate of Milton's intention.

In the prologues to *Paradise Lost*, as we have seen, Milton's poet repeatedly expresses his concern for sustaining an epic style answerable to the demands of his superhuman subject matter. This concern takes the shape of an admission of personal limitation and the corresponding need for divine guidance and support in his adventurous flight beyond the range of man's natural capacities. The poet realizes the potentially satanic posture his aspirations imply, and he attempts to counter such a potential in two ways; he emphasizes his properly dependent relation to God, and he tries to undercut the possibility of satanic error by displaying within his narrative his recognition that the danger of unwarranted presumption does in fact exist for a fallen man with his pretentions. The poet confesses his inadequacy for the task he has set himself, and only by insisting on this inadequacy does his relation to his subject remain decorous. This general attitude is expressed strikingly in the poet's final prologue. Here, as I have already noted, Milton points unequivocally to the limitations of former epic. But it is clear while he is doing this that the epic materials he describes as unworthy of the subject of man's revolt have been a part of his scheme. In this last direct address to his audience Milton seems almost to flaunt the fact that the very framework of his poem, a framework everywhere dependent on former epic, is not worthy of his subject which remains "sufficient of itself to raise / That name [heroic]" (IX, 43–44). As in the question of angelic armor, Milton chooses to probe a raw nerve which could more gracefully be fleshed over. This brazening of inadequacy can only be meant to convey one thing: in a fallen world one must build with fallen materials. The decorous style for the fallen poet of biblical epic cannot completely transcend epic tradition; it must rely on this tradition even when the tradition is sadly earthbound. The poet, in sum, cannot hope to answer a heavenly subject in heavenly terms, and one obvious way for him to avoid wandering into error is to keep this fact continually on display.

Within the narrative proper of *Paradise Lost* the central statement of the necessary discrepancy between transcendent subjects and a style suited to man's middle state is voiced by Milton's substitute narrator, Raphael:

> *High matter thou injoin's me, O prime of men,*
> *Sad task and hard, for how shall I relate*
> *To human sense th' invisible exploits*
> *Of warring Spirits; how without remorse*
> *The ruin of so many glorious once*
> *And perfet while they stood; how last unfold*
> *The secrets of another world, perhaps*
> *Not lawful to reveal? yet for thy good*
> *This is dispens't, and what surmounts the reach*
> *Of human sense, I shall delineate so,*
> *By lik'ning spiritual to corporal forms,*
> *As may express them best, though what if Earth*
> *Be but the shadow of Heav'n, and things therein*
> *Each to other like, more than on Earth is thought?*
> (V, 563–576)

This formula, corporeal forms to shadow spiritual, describes the method of much of *Paradise Lost*. But here the angel's poetic is specifically a description and tentative justification of the war in Heaven. According to Raphael, he will describe the war of angels in terms "As may express them best" to human understanding, and according to him a correspondence between these corporeal terms and his spiritual subject may exist in a sense yet uncomprehended. But Raphael makes no attempt to argue that corporeal forms will do anything like final justice to the description of "what surmounts the reach / Of human sense." On the contrary he apologizes for being forced to describe "invisible exploits" so grossly. Milton, it seems, has singled out this epic within an epic to delineate as sharply as possible the problem faced by the poet of superhuman events. Not only is the angelic war prefaced by Raphael's apology, it is concluded by a similar admission of metaphorical discrepancy ("Thus measuring things in Heav'n by things on Earth" [VI, 893]), and it is interspersed with repeated reminders of the awkwardness of Raphael's task:

> . . . *Regions to which*
> *All thy Dominion,* Adam, *is no more*
> *Than what this Garden is to all the Earth.*
> (V, 750–752)

> . . . *in the Dialect of men*
> *Interpreted . . . .*
> (V, 762–763)

> . . . *to set forth*
> *Great things by small . . . .*
> (VI, 310–311)

> . . . *as we compute the days in Heaven . . . .*
>   (VI, 586; this addressed to the Son!)

> . . . *for who, though with the tongue*
> *Of Angels, can relate, or to what things*
> *Liken on Earth conspicuous, that may lift*
> *Human imagination to such highth*
> *Of Godlike Power: for likest Gods they seem'd,*
> *Stood they or mov'd, in stature, motion, arms*
> *Fit to decide the Empire of great Heav'n.*
>   (VI, 297–303)

Such accommodating asides are not uncommon in *Paradise Lost*, as a glance at Books I and II will reveal, but here they cluster as the poet soars to such dizzy heights of visionary inquiry that he must end his flight with

> *Descend from Heav'n Urania . . . .*
>   *Up led by thee*
> *Into the Heav'n of Heav'ns I have presum'd,*
> *An Earthly Guest, and drawn Empyreal Air,*
> *Thy temp'ring; with like safety guided down*
> *Return me to my Native Element . . . .*
>   (VII, 1; 12–16)

Yet, to repeat, the higher the narrative of Books V and VI ascends into "the Heav'n of Heav'ns" the more grossly corporeal the descriptive style becomes. The reason for this, it seems to me, is that Milton is intent on exposing rather than concealing what Raphael has explained: that a style accommodated to human intelligence is inadequate to the demands of a heavenly narrative—that indeed, the acceptance of such inadequacy constitutes the

only proper decorum.[24] It was not, I think, enough for
Milton simply to announce, through Raphael, that the
subject of a heavenly war was essentially inexpressible.
Other poets had made such statements with a notable
lack of sincerity. Above all Milton did not wish to be
accused of presuming that his inflated Homerics were in
fact, all disclaimers aside, answering adequately to the
demands of his subject, and for this reason, it would
seem, he was willing to expose repeatedly the absurd
confusion of spirit and matter, Heaven and Earth, inherent in Raphael's basic metaphor.

Raphael begins his account of the war by echoing
Aeneas preparing to relate in the presence of Dido's court
his "Infandum . . . dolorem," the fall of Troy: "High matter thou injoin'st me, O prime of men, / Sad task and
hard" (V, 563–564). Milton here acknowledges a structural precedent for his retrospective narrative and, at the
same time, by obliquely comparing Satan's fall with
Troy's, he anticipates the traditional military mold in
which his heavenly action is to be cast. We need not
pause to verify Milton's often documented debt to former epic in these Books. Homer is his primary source,
and Newton's two-hundred-year-old description of the
poet's debt to Homer may warn us against excessive
demonstration:

[24] Louis Martz has briefly suggested that something like this
may have been Milton's intention: "The frequent stiffness and
clumsiness of the writing (along with the ponderous efforts at
witty irony) seem to result from a deliberate withholding of
Milton's full poetic power, in an effort to attenuate and ridicule
the heroic mode. It is a dangerous poetical strategy . . . ." *The
Paradise Within* (New Haven: Yale Univ. Press, 1964), p. 124.

It would be entering into too minute a detail of criticism, to mention every little circumstance that is copied from Homer. And, where he does not directly copy from Homer, his style and colouring are still very much in Homer's manner. Wonderful as his genius was, he could hardly have drawn the battles of Angels so well without first reading those in the Iliad . . . .[25]

With classical epic as a primary model Milton could not have hoped to avoid the materiality which so disturbed Johnson and subsequent critics. In the heavenly war force and weight inevitably become the primary measure of angelic deeds. As Raphael points out, such measurement is inaccurate, and as Raphael's narrative demonstrates, such measurement can become extremely grotesque. Corporeal descriptions awkwardly clog the spirituality of Heaven—spirituality which forms a part of the reader's expectation with respect to celestial things. Milton, his mortalism notwithstanding, confirms this expectation by prefacing the war with an unequivocal statement that in God's hierarchy the higher degrees are less solid, more spiritous:

> O Adam, *one Almighty is, from whom*
> *All things proceed, and up to him return*
> *If not deprav'd from good, created all*
> *Such to perfection, one first matter all,*
> *Indu'd with various forms, various degrees*
> *Of substance, and in things that live, of life;*
> *But more refin'd, more spiritous, and pure,*
> *As nearer to him plac't or nearer tending*
> *Each in thir several active Spheres assign'd*

[25] Newton, n. to VI, 239.

> *Till body up to spirit work, in bounds*
> *Proportion'd to each kind.*
>
> (V, 469–479)

This hierarchy in which matter is refined up to spirit is fundamental to Milton's ontology as, for example, Raphael's account of angelic lovemaking makes plain:

> *Whatever pure thou in the body enjoy'st*
> *(And pure thou wert created) we enjoy*
> *In eminence, and obstacle find none*
> *Of membrane, joint, or limb, exclusive bars:*
> *Easier than Air with Air, if Spirits embrace,*
> *Total they mix, Union of Pure with Pure*
> *Desiring . . . .*
>
> (VIII, 622–628)

The difficulty of describing in terms of traditional epic warfare the conflict of creatures who "obstacle find none / Of membrane, joint, or limb" is, to put it mildly, formidable. Yet that Raphael, after his introductory apologies, seems almost wantonly to ignore such difficulties needs very little demonstration. The most common and perhaps the least obtrusive kind of metaphorical awkwardness in Raphael's account arises, as in the following passage, from the attempt to describe angelic transcendence in terms of muscle:

> *So under fiery Cope together rush'd*
> *Both Battles main, with ruinous assault*
> *And inextinguishable rage; all Heav'n*
> *Resounded, and had Earth been then, all Earth*
> *Had to her Centre shook. What wonder when*
> *Millions of fierce encount'ring Angels fought*

> *On either side, the least of whom could wield*
> *These Elements, and arm him with the force*
> *Of all thir Regions: how much more of Power*
> *Army against Army numberless to raise*
> *Dreadful combustion warring, and disturb,*
> *Though not destroy, thir happy Native seat . . . .*
>   (VI, 215–26)

In attempting both to measure great by small and, at the same time, make this measurement in human terms, Raphael manages to describe a Heaven not more spiritual but infinitely more massive than Earth. The weakest angel here appears as a ponderous Titan capable of wielding all the world's elements. Matter, in this description, has not worked up to spirit but to greater matter.

In reading this passage, however, it is possible to forget what Milton has told us about the realms of matter and spirit, to simply accept a war of titans and let it go at that. But as in the case of angelic armor there are times when Milton will not allow us to make the best of a bad situation. For example, the simile which compares the marching army of God's angels to a flight of birds—a simile sometimes admired for its more than Homeric aptness—exhibits an inconsistency which cannot be ignored:

> *On they move*
> *Indissolubly firm; nor obvious Hill,*
> *Nor straitening Vale, nor Wood, nor Stream*
>   *divides*
> *Thir perfet ranks; for high above the ground*
> *Thir march was, and the passive Air upbore*
> *Thir nimble tread; as when the total kind*

> *Of Birds in orderly array on wing*
> *Came summon'd over* Eden *to receive*
> *Thir names of thee* . . . .
>
> (VI, 68–76)

Raphael's comparison, which lifts the advancing army into the air, seems at first an attempt to suggest angelic spirituality; but having recalled such expectations with respect to the nature of angels, the simile succeeds only in reminding us of the grotesqueness of the Homeric manner of Raphael's war. The momentary airiness of the angel's progress through the sky finally does nothing so much as to emphasize the solidity of the "ground" of Heaven with its obstructive hills, vales, woods, and streams which could serve, despite the insubstantiality of angelic "membrane, joint, or limb," to divide "Thir perfet ranks" "Indissolubly firm." Moreover, the oxymoronic "nimble tred" of their "march" born up by "the passive Air" does not finally have the effect of suggesting lightness. On the contrary it is more likely to recall the massive bulk of Satan rising from the burning lake, "aloft, incumbent on the dusky Air / That felt unusual weight" (I, 226–227).

In fact one of the most disturbing aspects of Raphael's heavenly war is that it so persistently echoes and amplifies the Homeric cast of Books I and II wherein epic heroics had seemed once and for all cast into the infernal pit. Milton perhaps prepares his reader for this recollection of Satan "incumbent on the dusky Air" by introducing the bird simile with another echo from Hell, the music in a *"Dorian* mood" (I, 550) which five books earlier had inspired the "temper" of the fallen angels:

> . . . *the Powers Militant*
> *That stood for Heav'n, in mighty Quadrate join'd*
> *Of union irresistible, mov'd on*
> *In silence thir bright Legions, to the sound*
> *Of instrumental Harmony that breath'd*
> *Heroic Ardor to advent'rous deeds . . . .*
>
> (VI, 61–66)

More obtrusive parallels between angelic warfare and infernal swashbuckling are easy to list: Satan's invention of cannon, for instance, and the Hesiodic description of the angel's retaliation in which "Hills amid the Air encounter'd Hills" (VI, 664) recall Moloch's hope to see "Black fire and horror shot with equal rage / Among . . . [God's] angels" (II, 67–68) and the demonic games wherein the participants, "with vast *Typhoean* rage . . . / Rend up both Rocks and Hills, and ride the Air / In whirlwind" (II, 539–541). In making Hell's heroics—heroics sadly characteristic of our fallen world—the metaphor of heavenly conflict, Raphael's attempt at accommodation appears clearly deficient, even to fallen minds, and if mock heroic ridicule is the intent of such deficiency, this ridicule, to repeat, casts its net to include the whole of Heaven. If Satan is comically deflated by his epic posturing, then even God, viewing his antagonists with Olympian irony or, like Achilles, lending his armor to a Patroclean Christ, is reduced by the comparison. Christ's glittering chariot no less than Satan's can bounce noisily "O'er Shields and Helms and helmed heads" (VI, 840), and while Homeric punning may be appropriate to corrupted angels, Raphael's final scatalogical jape—"Disburd'n'd Heav'n rejoiced, and soon repair'd / Her mural breach" (VI, 878–879)—cannot mock the devils without mocking Heaven at large. This climactic pun is as shocking and grotesque as any metaphysical extravagance, and one may prefer in reading it to discover a linguistically insensitive Milton rather than an indelicate one. I find it impossible not to credit Milton with conscious crudeness here, if for no other reason than the one Thomas Kranidas suggests: the purgation which concludes the "Intestine War in Heaven" (VI, 259) is consistent with a strain of metaphor which repeatedly offers us the rebel angels as violators of Heaven's vitals (See VI, 482–483; VI, 509–517; VI, 584–589).[26] The materiality and hence the inadequacy of Raphael's accommodation of things heavenly is perhaps epitomized by these violent organic metaphors. In them matter again has not worked up to spirit. Quite the contrary.

I cannot think Milton intended Heaven to be diminished by this stylistic indecorousness; the fault must lie where Raphael places it: in a poetic mode which in being forced to correspond to the capacities of Adam, of the reader, and of the fallen poet, must confess *and exhibit* its inability to answer ultimately to its subject. The general deflation of warlike heroism in *Paradise Lost* extends, I think, beyond heroics as a theme to heroics as a poetic style.

Given his biblical subject, the war in Heaven offered Milton his readiest opportunity to try his hand at the military pyrotechnics which bulked so large in the heroic tradition he sought with "no middle flight" to renovate.

[26] Thomas Kranidas, "A View of Milton and the Traditional," *Milton Studies*, 1 (1969), 15–29.

The frequent assumption that Milton chose here to compete with the poets of the past on their own terms is not,
to repeat, very circumspect since it totally ignores the fact
that in *Paradise Lost* Milton was attempting to shift the
terms of heroic argument to the "Subverting [of] worldly
strong" "by things deem'd weak" "and worldly wise / By
simply meek" (XII, 568–570). Such a conception of
Christian heroism suggests that Milton would not have
chosen to compete with Homer and Virgil by wielding a
heavier club. He was already armed with an "Argument
. . . sufficient of itself." The war in Heaven was, for him,
a chance not to out-Homer Homer but to match the methods of the Homeric tradition *against* his Christian argument and to display in this conjunction of style and subject the inadequacies of these methods. But, as I have
been arguing, such a display did not constitute a whole-
sale rejection of the pagan past. In a very real sense the
deficiencies of Raphael's Homeric mode are also the deficiencies of Milton the poet whose share in man's first
disobedience has condemned him to the use of fallen materials. Milton's attitude is paradoxical and is perhaps
most immediately accessible in his final prologue where
the problem of epic decorum is raised, directly, for the
last time. Here the poet, like Raphael before him, announces his "Sad task" and portrays himself, as we have
seen,

> *Not sedulous by Nature to indite*
> *Wars, hitherto the only Argument*
> *Heroic deem'd, chief maistry to dissect*
> *With long and tedious havoc fabl'd Knights*
> *In Battles feign'd; the better fortitude*

> *Of Patience and Heroic Martyrdom*
> *Unsung; or to describe Races and Games,*
> *Or tilting Furniture, emblazon'd Shields,*
> *Impresses quaint, Caparisons and Steeds;*
> *Bases and tinsel Trappings, gorgeous Knights*
> *At Joust and Tournament; the marshall'd Feast*
> *Serv'd up in Hall with Sewers, and Seneshals;*
> *The skill of Artifice or Office mean,*
> *Not that which justly gives Heroic name*
> *To Person or Poem. Mee of these*
> *Nor skill'd nor studious, higher Argument*
> *Remains, sufficient of itself to raise*
> *That name . . . .*

(IX, 27–44)

To understand Milton here one must notice first what I have already suggested: Milton specifically rejects only the *argument* of former epic. He is not rejecting out of hand epic structure or heroic style or even "tinsel Trappings" as useful descriptively, metaphorically, even parodically to his own "higher Argument." It does not take long to recall counterparts for most of his list of epic fripperies within *Paradise Lost*. Yet while we may qualify Milton's strictures in this prologue by noting that he condemns the materials of the heroic tradition as argument only, still their inferiority as argument implies their inferiority in general. In effect Milton is saying that while he wishes us to realize his critical attitude toward former epic, he must, of necessity, work within human tradition, he must speak the language of his fallen world. As Raphael, the angelic singer, must condescend to Adam, so the poet-prophet must comprehend his own vision in tra-

ditional forms—this makes him man. The point is essential for Milton; it is not just another example of humble
posturing; it is at once a critique and a vindication of the
humanist tradition.

IV

Raphael's Homeric epic pushes the grand style to the
point of bombast and beyond until its own inability to
cope with more than fallen grandeur is exposed. By contrast, the poetic style of Milton's other substitute narrator, Michael, is often considered to fail in its lack of
epic elevation and complexity. Yet in both cases much of
the critical discontent has arisen, I believe, from an un-
derestimation of Milton's concern to respond to his subject with a style answerable to his conception of the
Christian poet and the decorous Christian poem. As with
the inflated Homerics of Raphael's war, the poetic spareness of the final books of *Paradise Lost* answers to Milton's sense of decorum, here a decorum demanded by an
account of human history placed within a poem largely
prehistorical and cosmic in character. The style of Books
XI and XII indirectly constitutes Milton's final comment
on the poetics of *Paradise Lost*.

Negative responses to both the mood and style of
Books XI and XII have been frequent. In his study of the
paradise within, Louis Martz has both endorsed and explained such attitudes. He suggests, for one thing, that
in a poem which professes to be an assertion of eternal
Providence the final books present far too little in the
way of a positive demonstration of God's grace, and he
is surely right in finding such comforts as Michael offers

here more in the nature of abstract theology than they are lively evocations of divine love.[27] But it seems to me that to suggest Milton's emphasis on sin at the end of his epic constitutes in itself a failure in poetic strategy attacks much more than the final books of *Paradise Lost*. It attacks the Miltonic temperament generally—particularly as displayed in the later poems. Milton characteristically leaves us with a more emphatic vision of the evils we are heir to than of the grace which redeems us. The struggle with evil is primary in Milton's mind and the victory of grace, while it is always climactic, is also, paradoxically, understated. Evil and suffering occupy the foreground of Milton's two great poems of the fallen world: while Christ in *Paradise Regained* is not swayed by Satan's allurements, the harshness of his rejection of temptation emphasizes the agony of Christian warfare more than its glory; in victory Christ's standing, though it crucially contrasts man's falling, is a final posture which seems pointedly to frustrate any expectation of a conventional heroic act. Samson is similarly embattled, his triumph similarly muted—in this instance by the ambiguous and partial responses of his tribe to the report of his last hour. In his major epic, Milton's theological attitudes urged, as Martz concedes, a preponderance of evil at the end in order to insist that paradise was indeed lost. Adam's education occupies Books XI and XII, and because he is here fallen he can no longer know good by good; he can "know good only by means of evil."[28] Yet there is no reason why this theological disposition should produce bad poetry; it is, broadly speaking, the disposi-

[27] Martz, p. 150.
[28] *The Christian Doctrine*, C.E., XV, 115.

tion of the tragic poet, certainly the disposition of Milton as tragic poet: "for so in Physic things of melancholic hue and quality are us'd against melancholy, sour against sour, salt to remove salt humors."[29]

More damning than the charge that the final books fail as poetic strategy is the frequent dissatisfaction with the quality of the verse itself: "these two last books fall short of the sublimity and majesty of the rest"; "the actual writing in this passage is curiously bad"; "The voice of the bard and seer has lost its vigor, and the writing has become, at its worst, the Biblical paraphrase of an almost ordinary versifier."[30] The style has changed, and the alteration occupies the pole opposite to Raphael's military mode: syntax has relaxed, and the resounding sonority we have been taught to call Miltonic is generally absent. On occasion Milton returns to his earlier grand manner (the roll call of cities is an example) but here, as in the heavenly war, the style seems exaggerated, almost, as Stanley Fish has suggested, "to the extent . . . of self-parody, as if Milton were telling us that while spectacular effects are still within his scope, they are no longer necessary or desirable."[31] One cannot, I think, finish a reading of *Paradise Lost* without frequently feeling that the spareness of the final books—particularly of the last—is poetically inferior to what has gone before. But while the apparent relaxation of stylistic tension mars the close of Milton's poem, the final style of *Paradise Lost* is not, I

[29] Hughes' edition, p. 549.

[30] Respectively, Newton, 9th edn. (1790), n. to II, 446; C. S. Lewis, *A Preface to "Paradise Lost"* (London: Oxford Univ. Press, 1942), p. 125; Martz, p. 142.

[31] Fish, p. 301.

think, simply the result of fatigue or a loss of poetic power. Rather, as I have argued in the case of Raphael's heroic song, Milton's sense of a decorum suited to subject shapes his final poetic mode.

We can begin to understand the proprieties of Milton's style here by noticing a curious matter of detail. In Michael's version of future history at least two important devices of style, characteristic both of Raphael's narrative and of Milton generally, are employed either with sharply decreasing frequency or are dropped altogether: (1) the complex texture of classical allusion (much of it indirect) begins to fade in Book XI until in the flats of Book XII it has virtually vanished, and (2) nowhere in Michael's narrative does Milton call upon complex simile to enrich and elevate his style. These are notable omissions which contribute significantly to the altered style of Books XI and XII, and if we look back over *Paradise Lost* at Milton's primary purpose for employing simile and allusion we can see some design in their absence here.

Until the point of our parents' fatal disobedience in Book IX, the action of *Paradise Lost* has developed in settings which are to various degrees foreign to fallen man —Hell, Heaven, Chaos, the world's outer spheres, paradise—settings which the poet has been forced to accommodate to human understanding. The primary method of such accommodation is, as Raphael puts it, "measuring . . . by things on Earth" (VI, 893). Allusion to mankind's fallen past is one way in which Milton makes these measurements. His repeated comparison of the poem's action to the actions of classical epic is more than an entertaining poetic competition in which he seeks to demonstrate an ability to soar with more than Homeric or Virgilian

middle flight. In his use of allusion Milton is primarily
concerned to relate the unknown in terms of the known.
The militant angels are seen in terms of Homeric heroes.
To comprehend Raphael and Michael the reader is referred to Mercury. David and Orpheus, as we have seen,
are a part of the portrait of Adam as are, at various times,
Ulysses (IV, 301f.) and Aneneas.[32] Newborn Eve appears
as Narcissus, later as Venus (V, 55–57), Pandora (IV,
714), and Mary (V, 385; X, 183–184). In Hell scenes like
the building of Pandaemonium depend in part on the
reader's recollection of classical epic (*Aeneid*, I, 418–
440), and Satan himself is, of course, an amalgam of
classical heroes and villains. There is no need to document at length what any reader can verify for himself.
My point is only that Milton's allusiveness is a characteristic of style which is used to bring an alien subject matter within the range of the reader's literary experience.

Milton's epic similes are similarly a part of this attempt
to accommodate distant subjects to human understanding. Much recent critical appraisal of Milton's poetic
technique has concerned itself with showing that the effect of the Miltonic simile is often to open up the world
of the poem to the world of the audience.[33] In Hell, for
example, the leviathan simile and the comparison of the
floating devils to "Autumnal Leaves that strow the
Brooks / In Vallombrosa" (I, 302–303) achieve this effect in ways which can delight the analyst. Or, in the
case of paradise, the fallen world enters and renders the
unfallen world accessible not only in the familiar pas-

[32] See Harding, *The Club of Hercules*, p. 51.
[33] See for example Ferry, pp. 67–87; Martz, pp. 110–116; Fish,
pp. 1–56.

toral scene but in the similaic comparisons to such places as "that fair field / of *Enna*" and "that *Nyseian* Isle" (IV, 268–269; 275). Through a series of similes the evil of fallen Satan and a forecast of the fallen world gradually intrude themselves into Eden's perfection until, climactically, the Devil is compared to

> ... *one who long in populous City pent,*
> *Where Houses thick and Sewers annoy the Air,*
> *Forth issuing on a Summer's morn to breathe*
> *Among the pleasant Villages and Farms*
> *Adjoin'd, from each thing met conceives delight,*
> *The smell of Grain, or tedded Grass, or Kine,*
> *Or Dairy, each rural sight, each rural sound;*
> *If chance with Nymphlike step fair Virgin pass,*
> *What pleasing seem'd, for her now pleases more,*
> *She most, and in her look sums all Delight.*
> *Such Pleasure took the Serpent to behold*
> *This Flow'ry Plat, the sweet recess of* Eve . . . .
> (IX, 445–456)

With a bitter irony, the terms in which paradise can be understood by man's corrupted intelligence become themselves, within the poem's action, an anticipation of man's loss of innocence. Our perspective is, to our grief, Satan's.

Allusion and simile, then, are among the most obvious stylistic means employed by Milton to forge links between the world of his poem and his own world. They are also fundamental elements of the grand style at its most complex. The reason these elements are largely absent in Books XI and XII should be fairly obvious: here, the fallen world—previously the material of simile and

allusion—has become the matter proper of Michael's narrative. As Stanley Fish's perceptive analysis implies, the
poem's immediate reality descends in these final books
from the level of metaphysics to the mundane events of
man's history, and in this descent Christian history becomes for fallen man the primary image in amplification
of which much of the preceding drama of sin and virtue
can be recalled as archetypal metaphor.[34] In short, in the
final books the poetic priorities have been reversed: what
the reader has learned of the cosmos with the aid of mundane similitudes now operates to give metaphysical reso-
nance to his understanding of human history. These
resonances, as Fish argues, are an important part of the
reader's experience of the poem, but they remain only implicit in the text of Books XI and XII. They do not compli-
cate Michael's style by the intrusion of simile or direct
literary allusion because here the principal burden of the
angel's message—biblical history—is largely shaped, so
Milton thought, to the condition of the fallen reader.

In the final two books of *Paradise Lost* the poet finds
himself at last firmly rooted in a world which can be comprehended without the necessity of elaborate comparison.
To be sure, Adam in his ignorance needs occasional cor-
rection from Michael, but the reader, armed with his experience of the fallen world, is now on familiar ground.
Milton need no longer shock the reader with the repeatedly painful discovery that Hell is his own world intensi-
fied, or sadden him by a fallen view of Eden, or dislocate
him by the strain of comprehending Heaven in mundane
metaphors. A few reminders of classical epic remain in
Book XI, but they do not serve, as previously, to explain

[34] Fish, p. 296.

or vivify the subject at hand. Rather, in recalling scenes from the shields of Achilles and Aeneas, their primary function is to suggest precedents for the inclusion of futuristic vision in epic.[35] What has happened here is that in Michael's presentation of biblical history classical allusion and simile have become nonessential. Subjects which, because of their remoteness, have demanded all the poet's powers of comparison have disappeared, and in such a situation the only decorum consistent with what has gone before demands a withdrawal into a simpler style.

Of course Milton's tendency—particularly in Book XII —to lapse into meager biblical paraphrase cannot be explained away by any view of his poetic intention. But the obvious deletion of simile and allusion from Michael's poetry is too striking to be merely the result of haste or weariness or boredom. The loss of sonority and the relaxation of syntax could, perhaps, be explained in this way; but I rather think that these losses are also the result of a studied plainness. If, moreover, the demands of a decorum suited to Christian poetry are operating here, the style of these books comments indirectly on the nature of the Christian poet as Milton understood it. The comment is not, as Harold E. Toliver has argued, that the vision of "the historian rather than the 'creative' artist."[36] is finally proper for the fallen singer. The proprieties of Milton's style are not, to repeat, governed by a fluctuating sense

[35] See n. 13 above. Milton's only other obvious debt to pagan literature in Book XI is to Ovid's account of the flood, but here the attempt is certainly not to explain one mundane event in terms of another since in the Renaissance the floods described by Ovid and the Bible were not thought of as similar but as identical.

[36] "Complicity of the Voice in *Paradise Lost*," MLQ, 25 (1964), 170.

of purpose but by the nature of his subject. In his view, the function of the visionary poet was to minister, like the angels, between man and subjects sometimes beyond the scope of human comprehension. In the case of Raphael's military epic the subject was clearly "invisible to mortal sight" (III, 55). But with Michael's message to man, "those written Records pure" (XII, 513) of the fallen world, the matter was just as clearly within the range of his audience "though not but by the spirit understood" (XII, 514). This spirit, for Milton, was resident in every man, and while *Paradise Lost* is itself surely intended to aid the reader in his understanding of these "Records pure," it is appropriate that the poem should end not with a charged rhetorical persuasion but with an almost liturgical repetition of the facts of Christian history. Fish has remarked the anonymity of Michael's voice: "Unlike the epic voice, that great amphibian whose personal involvement complicates and enriches the discharging of his public obligation, the angel's individual presence is hardly felt . . . . his tone ranges from mild reproof to still milder approval."[37] Such a voice addresses appropriately not only Adam but also men of whom Milton could write, "no man or body of men in these times can be the infallible judges or determiners in matters of religion to any other men's consciences but their own."[38]

[37] Fish, p. 288.
[38] *A Tretise of Civil Power*, C.E., VI, 6. See above, p. 2.

4: An Imitation of the Son

I

THE LIKELIHOOD is great that a seventeenth-century poet undertaking a work as monumental as *Paradise Lost*, would have viewed his function in terms of the commonplace analogy articulated by Sidney in his *Defense*: the right poet resembles God. The creativity of God, Sidney records, is duplicated by the poet-maker who "disdaining to be tied to any . . . subjection, lifted up with the vigor of his own invention, doth grow in effect into another nature, in making things either better than Nature bringeth forth, or, quite anew, forms such as never were in Nature . . . ."[1] Don Cameron Allen, however, has warned us against the application of this commonplace to Milton:

The Renaissance traded in the market of analogy and one of its most valued illusions can be expressed in a formula: God is a poet and the world his poem: hence the poet is a god and

[1] Sir Philip Sidney, *Complete Works*, Albert Feuillerat, ed. (Cambridge: Cambridge Univ. Press, 1923), III, 8. Renaissance literary criticism is full of similar statements. See, for example, Tasso's well-known description of variety in epic: *Prose Diverse*, Cesare Guasti, ed. (Florence, 1875), I, 154–155. For a more general discussion see Bernard Weinberg, *A History of Literary Criticism in the Italian Renaissance* (Chicago: Univ. of Chicago Press, 1961), especially chapters 7 and 8.

his poetry a new world of his making. From this point of view
Milton detaches himself and returns to the more ancient tradition of Hesiod, Homer and the English Caedmon. The poet
is not god, for God himself is, through his intermediaries,
the source of all human song.[2]

Allen is far from wrong here, but his distinction is perhaps less radical than it may at first appear.

To begin with, few, if any, Renaissance poets or aes-
theticians would have denied that ultimately "God himself is . . . the source of all human song." Sidney again
speaks for many in carefully avoiding "too saucy a comparison" between God and the poet by giving "right
honor to the heavenly maker of that maker."[3] As Allen
suggests, it is essentially the sense that God, in his remoteness, must speak to man "through his intermediaries" that distinguishes Milton from those who, like
Sidney, maintained a buoyant confidence in "the zodiac
of . . . [man's] own wit." Milton, though he attempts
vastly more than a Sidney in the way of comprehending
Heaven, finds God distant, dwelling "in unapproached
Light" (III, 4), to be sought but never to be understood
essentially through the analogies of a fallen world. Milton, in sum, is closer than many Renaissance poets to the
tradition Hesiod, Homer, and Caedmon not in the almost
universal belief that God is the final source of all upright
singing but in his conviction that the poet, as a vessel of
God's word, can only speak through special mediation.
This fact, however, should not be construed to mean that
Milton divorced himself entirely from the tradition which

[2] Don Cameron Allen, *The Harmonious Vision* (Baltimore: Johns
Hopkins Press, 1954), p. xi.
[3] Sidney, III, 8.

viewed the poet's creative act as in some way analogous to the creativity of God. While Milton does not presume to imitate God, while he requires a Muse, he still looks to Heaven for a divine pattern of the Christian poet.

Not only God's remoteness but His self-sufficiency made Him finally inimitable for Milton. To function— even by analogy—after the manner of a God without equal, a God from whom all things emanate, would have involved the kind of claims made by Satan who is, in his own conception, an imitator of God. The Son of God, however, offered Milton an ideal pattern more easily and safely comprehended by the human poet,[4] and within *Paradise Lost* several broad similarities between the poet and the Son are clearly discernible. The broadest of these is the similarity between the poet and the Son as active agents of the divine will. In *Paradise Lost* the Son willingly obeys the Father and is ultimately dependent on Him; like the Son, the Christian poet of the prologues— in ways not at all surprising—seeks also to serve by freely becoming an obedient agent of God's providential plan. More specifically, Milton displays the Son as the primary agent of all accommodations of God's mystery: "in him all his Father shone / Substantially express'd" (III, 139–140); thus the Son, in his mediatorial office, serves in part as a prophet for mankind[5]—a role to which

[4] This has not gone unrecognized. See especially B. Rajan, "Simple, Sensuous and Passionate," *RES*, 21 (1945), 289–301; John T. Shawcross, "The Metaphor of Inspiration in *Paradise Lost*," *Th' Upright Heart and Pure*, Amadeus P. Fiore, ed. (Pittsburgh: Dusquesne Univ. Press, 1967), pp. 75–85; and Ira Clark, "Milton and the Image of God," *JEGP*, 68 (1969), 422–431.

[5] The mediatorial office of Christ is discussed in *The Christian Doctrine*, Book I, chs. 5 and 15.

the poet, attempting to reveal to men "things invisible to mortal sight" (III, 55), likewise aspires. Finally, with reference to the traditional God-maker/poet-maker analogy, the Son effects the world's creation, a creative act ultimately inspired by God. In Milton's mind, as I hope to show, the poet's creative act is analogous to this great manifestation of God's love.

Milton's choice of the Son as a model for the poet of *Paradise Lost* involved, of course, more than an alteration of the tradition of Christian poetics. As Milton had recorded years before, his poetic vocation and his life were inseparable,[6] and for him, as for all Christians, the proper pattern for human activity lay in the example of the Son of God. C. A. Patrides, in his recent study of Milton's relation to Christian tradition, is one of many to emphasize the importance of the *Imitatio Christi* for Milton's age:

Milton's contemporaries judged these "rudiments" [the fundamental aspects of Christ's life and achievement] to be of supreme practical significance to the lives of men. The God-man was designated invariably as the most perfect exemplar of the conduct expected of all men, "our patterne," "a patterne to vs how we ought to walk," "our Teacher by his words, and Accomplisher by his deeds."[7]

For Milton himself, however, "our patterne" does not seem limited to the worldly "rudiments" of Christ's life. The Puritan mentality, as Louis L. Martz has argued, was drawn more to the aspect of the Son in his providential offices than to his role as passionate sufferer, more "to his

[6] See *The Reason of Church Government*, C.E., III.1, 303.
[7] C. A. Patrides, *Milton and the Christian Tradition* (Oxford: The Clarendon Press, 1966), p. 146.

official role than to his personality,"[8] and the evidence of
Milton's epic suggests that this interest shaped in part
Milton's sense of the Son as an object of imitation. It can,
of course, be objected that in fact the Son's "official" role
was unique and therefore inimitable, and in a strict sense
this is surely true—particularly with respect to the Son's
offices of priest and king. But despite the Son's uniqueness it would be clearly wrong to suggest that either
Paradise Lost or, more generally, orthodox Christian doctrine implies that no aspect of the Son's "official" role
can be imitated by mankind. Both the Bible and Milton's
poem are full of anticipations and imitations of Christ's
mediatorial office.[9] The Son's prophetic function, as I
have just suggested, was taken up by Milton as it had
been taken up by many before him, and while mankind
clearly could not, in Milton's mind, redeem itself, the
Son's sacerdotal offer to intercede for fallen man—an
offer voiced in Heaven ("on mee let thy anger fall" [III,
237; see XI, 25–44]) and echoed in Eden by our fallen
parents (X, 828–841; 933–936)—serves in *Paradise Lost*
as a pattern for man's regeneration.[10] As we have seen,

[8] Louis L. Martz, *The Poetry of Meditation*, 2nd ed. (New Haven:
Yale Univ. Press, 1962), p. 163. Martz is quoting Helen C. White,
English Devotional Literature, 1600–1640, University of Wisconsin
Studies in Language and Literature, No. 29 (Madison: Univ. of
Wisconsin Press, 1931), p. 195.

[9] Milton's description of Christ in *The Christian Doctrine*—"he
is the one mediator between God and man" (C.E., XIV, 191)—
would seem to indicate that Christ is the only mediator. This is
misleading. Typologically there are, in Milton's mind, other medi-
ators: "The name and office of mediator is in a certain sense
ascribed to Moses, as a type of Christ" (C.E., XV, 18–19).

[10] While the Son's offer is made in Heaven, Milton, in *The
Christian Doctrine*, sees Christ's redemptive act as representative

in Milton's epic the shape of providence is stamped on our sublunary world. The Son incarnates himself to become our redeemer and "our patterne"; yet his human perfection remains a shadow of his divine nature, and in consequence Milton, envisioning an ultimate model for the poet and for mankind, looks to the example of the Son in both his divine and human aspects. To so consider the scope of the poet's imitation of the Son in *Paradise Lost* can help us to understand the nature of Milton's attempt at divine epic.

II

Let us begin with the Son as he appears in *Paradise Lost*: centrally he is God's agent and the primary expression of God's accommodation of the divine mode to His greater and lesser creatures. This conception is repeatedly emphasized in passages which describe a Son "in whose face" the invisible Father "is beheld / Visibly" (VI, 681–682), a Son who expresses what in the Father cannot otherwise be understood (see also III, 138–141; III, 169–170; X, 65–67).[11] Milton had made clear years before in *Of Education* the relevance for man of such a visible expression of God:

The end of learning is to repair the ruins of our first parents by regaining to know God aright, and out of that knowledge

---

of the Savior "more particularly in his human nature" (C.E., XIV, 293).

[11] Similar statements appear in *The Christian Doctrine* (see especially C.E., XIV, 233, 265). The issue of Milton's alleged Arianism, while important and very complex, need not intrude here on Milton's basic conception in *Paradise Lost* of an accommodating Son. The extensive literature on Milton and Arianism has been recently reviewed in Patrides, pp. 15–25.

to love him, to imitate him, to be like him, as we may the nearest by possessing our souls of true virtue, which being united to the heavenly grace of faith makes up the highest perfection. But because our understanding cannot in this body found itself but on sensible things, nor arrive so clearly to the knowledge of God and things invisible as by orderly conning over the visible and inferior creature, the same method is necessarily to be followed in all discreet teaching.

(C.E., IV, 277)

In *Paradise Lost*, even before the fall, Adam is made aware of such an educational process:

> *O favorable Spirit, propitious guest,*
> *Well hast thou taught the way that might direct*
> *Our knowledge, and the scale of Nature set*
> *From centre to circumference, whereon*
> *In contemplation of created things*
> *By steps we may ascend to God.*

(V, 507–512)

Thus according to Milton, the progress of man's knowledge moves from the understanding of lesser things to greater, but, as the passages describing the Son as a "visible" expression of the "invisible" Father insist, this progress inevitably fails to comprehend God directly. In *Paradise Lost* even the angels see only the dark skirts of the Father, "Thron'd inaccessible." "To know God aright, to imitate him" is to know and imitate His "visible" accommodations, the first of which is manifest in the Son, incarnate as Christ and as represented in scriptural record. This is what fallen Adam learns from his pre-scriptural revelation of the world restored: to be "Taught . . . by his example whom I now / Acknowledge my Redeemer ever blest" (XII, 572–573).

The Son, then, appears within the action of Milton's epic as an exemplar. He serves as a model for man to imitate in his attempt to regain the "Divine similitude" which, as Michael explains to Adam, sin has disfigured (XI, 512). The extent to which Milton himself, "fall'n on evil days" (VII, 25), looks to this model can be observed by examining again the complex associations which surround the poet of the prologues. Many of these associations find their ultimate relevance in a comparison of the poet to the Son as he is described within the poem itself.

III

Milton begins *Paradise Lost* with an appeal to Heaven:

> *Sing Heav'nly Muse, that on the secret top*
> *Of* Oreb, *or of* Sinai, *didst inspire*
> *That Shepherd, who first taught the chosen Seed*
> *In the Beginning how the Heav'ns and Earth*
> *Rose out of* Chaos: *Or if* Sion *Hill*
> *Delight thee more, and* Siloa's *Brook that flow'd*
> *Fast by the Oracle of God; I thence*
> *Invoke thy aid to my advent'rous Song* . . . .
>   (I, 6–13)

The poet here associates himself with Moses who, though "slow of speech, and of a slow tongue" (Exodus 4:10), became through divine inspiration the prophetic leader of his race. Moses was, of course, considered among the first Old Testament types of Christ, and the poet, by linking himself with the first lawgiver, suggests ultimately a comparison with the incarnate redeemer who fulfills "The Law of God . . . / Both by obedience and by love, though love / Alone fulfill the Law" (XII, 402–404).[12] Milton's reference to "*Sion* Hill," the mount of prophecy and revelation, reemphasizes his placement of the poet in the prophetic line which culminates in Christ at the same time that it suggests a more complex parallel between the poet and the Son of God. "If Earth / Be but the shadow of Heaven," as Raphael speculates in Book V (574–575), then the Son who becomes God's anointed on Heaven's "holy Hill" (V, 604) is the divine substance of which those prophets exalted by God on "*Sion* Hill" are the shadows. Milton's Pauline interpretation of the second Psalm in *The Christian Doctrine* (C.E., XIV, 182–185) makes it clear that he considered the hill upon which God "begets" the Son and upon which, in *Paradise Lost*, the Son becomes God's effective mediator between Heaven and Earth to be the heavenly archetype of Sion. When, therefore, the poet calls his Muse from "*Sion* Hill" he is not only aligning himself with the prophets; by obliquely associating his own desire to become the vessel of God's mediation with the Messiah's exaltation on Heaven's "holy Hill," he looks toward the example of the Son in Heaven as his ultimate aspiration. Thus Milton begins *Paradise Lost* by desiring to be exalted by God as a servant of mankind; his ultimate model for this posture is the Son in both his earthly and heavenly aspects.

[12] See *The Christian Doctrine*: "Under the name of CHRIST are also comprehended Moses and the Prophets, who were his forerunners" (C.E., XIV, 19). The verse from Exodus and these lines from *Paradise Lost* are related similarly in Shawcross, "The Metaphor of Inspiration," p. 77.

In his heavenly aspect the Son stands at the head of the angelic hierarchy. As early as the Nativity Ode Milton had looked to angelic song as the divine pattern for the earthbound poet's utterances, and in *Paradise Lost* the angels, in their song and in their ministering to man's ignorance of God's ways, remain, as we have seen, closely parallel to Milton's conception of the Christian poet's function. As with the poet/prophet association, angelic models for the poet point finally to the Son.

It will be recalled from the preceding chapter that one of the more striking ways in which Milton calls attention to such similarities between the poet and the angels of *Paradise Lost* is through the imagery of light. Light, in *Paradise Lost*, is Milton's central metaphor for God's creative love; it represents all goodness that emanates from God who "is Light"; it figures all His accommodations to those who are not God. In the poem these accommodations are frequently manifest in and through the angels who are, as we have seen, called "Sons of Light" (V, 160; XI, 80). Uriel, the poem's first angelic "Interpreter" (III, 657) of God and its first singer of creation (III, 708–734), is complexly associated with light (III, 663ff.); God's minister, Raphael, descending to Paradise to shed light upon light appears in Eden like "another Morn / Ris'n on mid-noon" (V, 310–311); and fallen man's first angelic minister, Michael, is similarly brilliant (XI, 206), but he finds himself, like the poet Milton, in a darkened world (XI, 204). Thus, to relate the poet's ministry and song to angelic models, Milton describes the poet functioning, like the angels, as a lens for God's light. Like the angels, the visionary poet both receives and projects the goodness of God's ways:

> Hail holy Light, offspring of Heav'n first-born,
> Or of th' Eternal Coeternal beam
> May I express thee unblam'd? . . . .
>   thee I revisit safe,
> And feel thy sovran vital Lamp . . . .
>   (III, 1–3; 21–22)

As with the angels and the poet, the Son's relationship to God is described by the symbol of light. Standing nearest to God, he represents the first example of the effect of God's light on His greater and lesser creatures:

> . . . in him all his Father shone . . . .
>   (III, 139)

> [The Son] On his great Expedition now appear'd,
> Girt with Omnipotence, with Radiance crown'd
> Of Majesty Divine, Sapience and Love
> Immense, and all his Father in him shone.
>   (VII, 192–195)

> Begotten Son, Divine Similitude,
> In whose conspicuous count'nance, without cloud
> Made visible, th' Almighty Father shines,
> Whom else no creature can behold . . . .
>
>   (III, 384–387)

God's light shines *in* the Son; the Son makes visible what God is. Like the poet, like the angelic models of the poet, the Son functions as an accommodating lens, receiving the divine effluence and directing it toward creatures less blessed. Thus when in *Paradise Lost* Milton alludes to light as a sign of God's relationship to one of His creatures, he sets up a chain of association which ascends toward the Son. The blind poet, as he appears in the four prologues to the epic, is a crucial link in this chain:

> *So much the rather thou Celestial Light*
> *Shine inward, and the mind through all her powers*
> *Irradiate, there plant eyes, all mist from thence*
> *Purge and disperse, that I may see and tell*
> *Of things invisible to mortal sight.*
>
> (III, 51–55)

IV

We can say, then, that the poet of *Paradise Lost* resembles the Son in his desire to minister prophetically to fallen mankind's needs; his epic seeks to illuminate human darkness. The question, however, remains: does the poet/Son analogy end here where, roughly speaking, it might be said to extend to most conscientious Christian poets? As I have suggested, the answer is no. Milton pursues the analogy between the poet-maker and the Son by recalling in Book VII that it is the Messiah who is, in effect, the artist of the universe, God's creative agent, His Word. *Paradise Lost*, as I wish to show, offers us evidence that Milton considered the creative acts of the Son to be dimly shadowed by the creative acts of the poet. This evidence consists in part of a developed parallel between their respective creations, between the order of *Paradise Lost* and the order of the world.

Milton's sense of his universe derives ultimately from a Pythagorean-Platonic conception of world order, a conception emphasizing a rational, musical, mathematical structure which could stand as a model for all other structures—intellectual and artistic. In the Middle Ages on through the Renaissance, aesthetic theory, under the influence of Augustine for one, had frequent recourse to the idea that the work of art—the musical composition, the painting, the building, the poem—should emulate the harmonious proportions of God's own artifact, the world.[13] From his second prolusion where "Father Pythagoras" and "The greatest of Mother Nature's interpreters, Plato" are exalted above mundane Aristotle, to the description of creation in *Paradise Lost*, Milton consistently returns to the idea that *music* and *measure* describe both the divinely created object and the divinely creative act. The world, its dark foundations cast deep, is in Milton's description a vast edifice designed by the "sovran Architect" (V, 256; see VIII, 73) and accomplished by his compass-wielding Son. At the same time the world is a great harmonious symphony:

> *Ring out ye Crystal spheres*
> *Once bless our human ears,*
> > *(If ye have power to touch our senses so)*
> *And let your silver chime*
> *Move in melodious time;*
> > *And let the Bass of Heav'n's deep Organ blow,*

[13] The tradition of these ideas of world order and art has been traced often enough to need no detailed description here. In particular see Ernst Robert Curtius, *European Literature and the Latin Middle Ages*, trans. Willard Trask (New York: Pantheon Books, 1953); Otto von Simson, *The Gothic Cathedral* (New York: Pantheon Books, 1954); Rudolf Wittkower, *Architectural Principles in the Age of Humanism* (London: Alec Tiranti, 1952); Erwin Panofsky, *Meaning in the Visual Arts* (Garden City, N. Y.: Doubleday, 1955).

> *And with your ninefold harmony*
> *Make up full consort to th' Angelic symphony.*
> > (Nativity Ode: 125–132)

From his earliest utterances on poetry, Milton's expressed desire was to emulate such harmonies,

> *As once we did, till disproportion'd sin*
> *Jarr'd against nature's chime, and with harsh din*
> *Broke the fair music that all creatures made*
> *To their great Lord, whose love their motion*
> > *sway'd*
> *In perfect Diapason . . . .*
> > ("At a Solemn Music": 19–23)

The evidence, as I see it, suggests that *Paradise Lost* represented for Milton at least a partial fulfillment of this desire. However, the ways in which Milton attempts in his epic to emulate the divine order of things deserve careful scrutiny.

In Christian versions of the Pythagorean-Platonic world order, number, as Ernst Robert Curtius has written, was "sanctified as a form-bestowing factor in the divine work of creation."[14] In consequence one way in which medieval and Renaissance poets could attempt to echo heavenly harmony was through a mathematically proportioned structure, and in recent years several suggestions have been made, notably by Gunnar Qvarnström, John Shawcross, and Alastair Fowler, with regard to a symmetrical structure in *Paradise Lost*.[15] Some of

---

[14] Curtius, p. 504.

[15] Gunnar Qvarnström, *The Enchanted Palace* (Stockholm: Almqvist and Wiksell, 1967); John T. Shawcross, "The Balanced Structure of *Paradise Lost*," *SP*, 63 (1965), 696–718; *The Poems of*

these suggestions are very conjectural, but the conclusion offered by all three of these critics that Milton's epic is structured around a thematic center which is numerologically placed seems almost inescapable. In the 1667 edition of *Paradise Lost* the central event is the ascension of the Son into the chariot of the Father (VI, 760–763; 1674 ed.), a theologically crucial moment which occurs at the exact midpoint of the poem. In Milton's 1674 revision this central peripety is replaced, according to Fowler, by "the 'episode' of Raphael" (V–VIII) which, balancing the Son's wrathful triumph (VI) against his merciful creation (VII), forms a structural core around which the remaining books, considered in terms of their subjects, group themselves symmetrically.[16] These observations are persuasive enough in their details to suggest, at least, that Milton was in some measure concerned with numerological structure and, in natural consequence of the rationale for such structures, viewed himself as an imitator of divine patterns. However, if such concerns

---

John Milton, John Carey and Alastair Fowler, eds. (London: Longmans, 1968). The idea that Milton was interested in numerology has also been explored by Maren-Sofie Röstvig, *The Hidden Sense* (New York: Humanities Press, 1963) and James Whaler, *Counterpoint and Symbol*, *Anglistica*, 4 (Copenhagen: Rosenkilde and Bagger, 1956).

[16] Carey and Fowler, pp. 442–443: 'The outermost two books in each case are concerned with the consequences of a fall: i–ii portray the evil consequences of the fall of the angels, xi–xii the mixed consequences of the Fall of man. Next comes a divine council of deliberation on man's fall, and Christ's offer of mediation (iii), this is answered by a council of judgment, and by Christ's descent to judge and clothe fallen man (x). Similarly, in iii Satan enters the universe, in x he leaves it. Bk iv has the first temptation, which is answered in ix by the second."

were in fact Milton's, they do not, I feel, represent him operating from the strengths of his particular talent. More attractive and somewhat less speculative evidence of Milton's sense of his creative role is available.

Neither for Milton nor for Renaissance poets generally did the analogy between poem and cosmos depend exclusively on number. For some inspiration was an easier means than mathematics to the perception of divine harmonies. Cowley, anticipating Milton's attempt at a biblical epic in English, is a case in point:

> *Tell me, oh* Muse *(for* Thou, *or none canst tell*
> *The mystick pow'rs that in blest* Numbers *dwell,*
> *Thou their great* Nature *know'st, nor is it fit*
> *This noblest Gem of thine own Crown t' omit)*
> *Tell me from whence these heav'nly charms arise;*
> *Teach the dull world* t' admire *what they* despise.[17]

These are the first lines of the invocation to *Davideis*, an invocation (complete with a weighty footnote) which could serve as a compendium of the general notions of art and universal harmony available to a Renaissance poet. Cowley touches first upon "blest *Numbers*" as the key to the proportions of "*Gods Poem*," but his sense of a correspondence between "this *Worlds* new *Essay*" and his own epic is based on nothing so exact as mathematical symmetry or specific number symbolism. In presenting a world/poem analogy Cowley ultimately depends on a generalized conception of harmony as the basis of all order. Music and dance figure heavenly harmony, and poetry is fused to these as an harmonious art. Milton

[17] Abraham Cowley, *Poems*, A. R. Waller, ed. (Cambridge: Cambridge Univ. Press, 1905), p. 253.

frequently recurs to this kind of simple equation of poetry or verbal eloquence with the other harmonious arts—particularly music—which in their ordering of sound, motion, or matter can be viewed as loosely analogous to God's harmonious creation. At the end of his prolusion on the harmony of the spheres, for instance, the true model for oratorical style becomes, by a comparison, the heavenly harmony he has been expounding (C.E., XII, 157). In *Arcades*, to cite a more familiar example, the poet aspires to the formative music which issues from Heaven:

> *Such sweet compulsion doth in music lie,*
> *To lull the daughters of Necessity,*
> *And keep unsteady Nature to her law,*
> *And the low world in measur'd motion draw*
> *After the heavenly tune, which none can hear*
> *Of human mold with gross unpurged ear;*
> *And yet such music worthiest were to blaze*
> *The peerless height of her immortal praise,*
> *Whose luster leads us, and for her most fit,*
> *If my inferior hand or voice could hit*
> *Inimitable sounds . . . .*

$$(68-78)$$

The record of such aspirations as these should inform our reading of the invocations to *Paradise Lost*. When in Book III Milton displays the poet feeding "on thoughts, that voluntary move / Harmonious numbers" (III, 37–38), he is referring to much more than an effort to write sonorous verse; he refers more inclusively to a conception of poetry as an echo of God's created harmony. Unlike Cowley's erudition, Milton's learning is not trotted out ostentatiously and verified in footnotes. He assumes

in his "fit audience" knowledge roughly correspondent
to his own, knowledge which will allow a fleeting reference to the traditional analogy between poem and cosmos
to stand for a great deal. Such references are an important feature of *Paradise Lost*, and they point more
surely than any guess regarding numerological composition to Milton's conception of the poet's imitation of
divine creativity.

Milton implies from the outset that the writing of
Paradise Lost is in some sense analogous to God's creation
of the world by invoking as Muse that same Spirit who

> *. . . from the first*
> *Wast present, and with mighty wings outspread*
> *Dove-like satst brooding on the vast Abyss*
> *And mad'st it pregnant.*

> (I, 19–22)

Many critics have attempted to identify the precise theological nature of this Muse whom Milton inconveniently
cloaked in various guises: the Dove, Light, Urania, "my
celestial Patroness."[18] The problem is by no means simple,

---

[18] The central antagonists in the by now traditional controversy
over the identification of Milton's Muse are Harris F. Fletcher, *Milton's Rabbinical Readings* (Urbana: Univ. of Illinois Press, 1930)
and Maurice Kelley, *This Great Argument* (Princeton: Princeton
Univ. Press, 1941). Fletcher supports the identification of the Muse
with the third member of the Trinity. Kelley's rebuttal is currently
the orthodox view: "when John Milton sought divine guidance for
his supreme poetical effort, he addressed a Muse who is separate
and apart from the Third Person of the Trinity . . . . [he] turned for
inspiration and knowledge not to what he considered a subordinate
figure but rather to the Father himself—the very fountain-head of
all wisdom and enlightenment" (pp. 117–118). More detailed sum-
maries of commentary on Milton's Muse are available in Kelley,

but before we reject the unity of the Muse or undertake
to show that Milton was in fact invoking the Holy Ghost
or the Messiah himself, we should, I think, be forewarned
by the fact that Milton made no such overt identifications
in his poem. As he tells us in the prologue to Book VII, he
is interested in "the meaning, not the Name," and his
descriptions of his Muse in the invocations offer considerable evidence as to what kinds of meanings a heavenly
Muse embodied for him. The passage just quoted from
the first invocation to *Paradise Lost* centers on one primary attribute of Milton's Muse: knowledge and influence in the matter of the world's creation. Milton begins
his major act of poetic creation by asking the Spirit he
associates with God's creative acts to preside over his
own work. A poem/cosmos analogy is clearly implicit
in this.

Again in Book VII Milton invokes a Muse wise in the
ways of God's ordering of chaos—this time to assist in
the poet's own account of the first week. The Muse's
name, Urania, which Milton tells us is important for its
associative meanings, was, as Lily Bess Campbell has
reminded us,[19] assigned by Du Bartas and Spenser not
just to a pagan muse of astronomy but to a patroness of
hexaemeral knowledge. Thus Urania, "The meaning, not
the Name," is a Muse altogether proper to the subject of
Book VII, but it should also be noticed that in his invocation to this book Milton does not simply request aid in

---

pp. 109–118 and Jackson I. Cope, *The Metaphoric Structure of
"Paradise Lost"* (Baltimore: Johns Hopkins Press, 1962), pp.
148–150.

[19] Lily Bess Campbell, "The Christian Muse," *Huntington Library Bulletin* (Oct., 1935), pp. 29–70.

describing God's creative week. It is Urania who has led the poet "Into the Heav'n of Heav'ns" (VII, 13), who will (so he hopes) return him safely to his own "Native Element" (VII, 16), and who will continue to aid him in the "Half" of his epic that "yet remains unsung" (VII, 21). We can see, then, that here, as in the first invocation, Milton is calling as Muse a heavenly Spirit associated with the creation to preside over the *whole* of *Paradise Lost*.

In Raphael's account of the first week within Book VII proper the relation of Milton's Muse to the mechanisms of the world's creation are more specifically revealed. Milton has begun his epic, as we have seen, by calling forth the dovelike Spirit who "with mighty wings outspread / . . . satst brooding on the vast Abyss." This is the Spirit of Genesis who "moved [brooded] upon the face of the deep."[20] While there is some conflicting testimony in *The Christian Doctrine* as to the identity of this Spirit, the fact that in his treatise Milton forbids the invocation of the third person of the Trinity and, in describing the creation, insists that the Spirit is God's "divine power rather than any person" (C.E., X, 13) makes it very unlikely that the Spirit is to be identified either as the Holy Ghost or the Son.[21] In *Paradise Lost*, moreover, Raphael's

[20] *Brooded* is an alternative translation of Genesis 1:2, which Milton obviously credited. In *The Christian Doctrine* he translates the word *incubabat*.

[21] See Kelley, p. 112n. At one point in *The Christian Doctrine* (C.E., XIV, 359–361) Milton seems to associate the Spirit of Genesis 1:2 with the Son. Later (C.E., XV, 13) he maintains that the Spirit is no member of the Trinity but God's divine power. Kelley is "disposed to follow this second interpretation because it is Milton's most complete exposition of the passage, because Milton declares that he had so interpreted it in the earlier chapter of his

version of the creation appears clearly to describe this Spirit as separate from the Son. Before the Son voyages into chaos on his mission of creation, he is told by the Father, "My overshadowing Spirit and might *with thee /* I send along" (VII, 165–166; my emphasis). It seems almost without question that this is the same Spirit who appears a few lines later:

> *Darkness profound*
> *Cover'd th' Abyss: but on the wat'ry calm*
> *His brooding wings the Spirit of God outspread,*
> *And vital virtue infus'd, and vital warmth*
> *Throughout the fluid Mass . . . .*
>
> (VII, 233–237)

Based, then, simply on the information offered by Milton in *Paradise Lost* this much ought to be plain with regard to the identification of the poet's Muse: (1) the Muse of the initial invocation is indistinguishable from the "Spirit of God" who in Book VII "on the wat'ry calm" "outspread" "His brooding wings";[22] (2) this "overshadow-

---

treatise, and because this seems the interpretation present in P.L., VII, 165–166." One should, however, see William B. Hunter, Jr., "The Meaning of Holy Light in *Paradise Lost*," *MLN*, 74 (1959), 589–592. Hunter identifies holy Light with the Son.

[22] There is, perhaps, a problem of gender here. The Muse is usually described as feminine in the prologues. Within the narrative of Book VII the Spirit is referred to by a masculine pronoun. The fact of the matter would seem to be what John Shawcross suggests ("The Metaphor of Inspiration"): the Spirit of Genesis which both broods and impregnates is androgynous. It is surely this androgynous Spirit who appears as Muse in Milton's first invocation and again as the Spirit of God in Book VII: "His brooding wings." To see Milton's Muse as protean in nature is not necessarily to deny her unity (see below).

ing Spirit" is sent along with the Son and is therefore,
presumably, not identical with him. Such a reading adds
a rich dimension to Milton's modeling of the poet after
the example of the Son as God's creative agent. The poet,
in his invocations, requests guidance from the same Spirit
who has accompanied the Messiah on his mission of
creation. Both the poet (hopefully) and the Son (in
the poet's understanding of him) create for the benefit of
mankind as agents of God's Spirit—a protean Spirit, it
would seem from Milton's addresses to her, but a Spirit
unified both by the omnipresence of God Who sends her
forth and by her function in *Paradise Lost* of presiding
over the acts of creation—poetic and universal.

V

As noted in Chapter I, we need look no further than
Marvell's dedicatory poem to find testimony that in an
undertaking as momentous as *Paradise Lost* the poet's
imitation of divine creativity would have been taken for
granted by a seventeenth-century reader:

> *Thy verse created like thy theme sublime,*
> *In Number, Weight, and Measure, needs not Rime.*

The "theme sublime" here is the world's foundation, and
the phrase, "Number, Weight, and Measure" is borrowed
from a verse in the Book of Wisdom which was central
in delivering into Christian hands the Pythagorean-
Platonic notions of order that were to shape the medieval
world view. Solomon's words, "thou hast ordered all
things in measure, number, and weight" (Wisdom of
Solomon, 11:12), were widely considered to constitute

not only a description of God's command for the construction of the great Hebraic temple but also an indica-
tion of God's own creative method.[23] Marvell's allusion
to this apocryphal passage and by implication to the
aesthetic it helped foster is, as I have already suggested,
far from idle in a discussion of Milton's epic. The Temple
of Solomon and its implications for the human arts are
on Milton's mind from the first. His Muse is not only a
Spirit associated with the world's creation; she also de-
lights in Sion Hill where Solomon built in imitation of
God's handiwork, and corresponding to her association
with the site of the Temple, she is "chiefly Thou O Spirit,
that dost prefer / Before all Temples th' upright heart
and pure" (I, 17–18).[24] These lines present a radical shift
in categories—from architecture to the human heart—
which is rich in its implications and perhaps, for a secular
age, in need of a gloss.

To Milton's contemporary audience the comparison of
the Temple to the heart was traditional and depended on
the Christian conception of man—his body or heart or
soul—as the temple of the Lord (I Corinthians, 3:9–17).
Milton unfolds this concept in some of its variety in
The Reason of Church Government:

Did God take such delight in measuring out the pillars, arches
and doores of a materiall Temple, was he so punctuall and
circumspect in lavers, altars, and sacrifices soone after to be
abrogated, lest any of these should have been made contrary

[23] For discussions of the importance of this verse in medieval
and Renaissance thought see Curtius, pp. 501–509; von Simson,
pp. 21–29; and Wittkower, pp. 121–126.

[24] See Shawcross, "The Metaphor of Inspiration": "In a way, I
suppose, Milton's poem becomes his temple for God's covenant"
(p. 77).

to his mind? is not a farre more perfect worke more Agreeable
to his perfection in the most perfect state of the Church
militant, the new alliance of God to man? should not he rather
now by his owne prescribed discipline have cast his line and
levell upon the soule of man which is his rationall temple, and
by the divine square and compasse thereof forme and regenerate in us the lovely shapes of vertues and graces, the
sooner to edifie and accomplish the immortall stature of
Christs body which is his Church in all her glorious lineaments and proportions.

(C.E., III.1, 191)

Here the comparison of the human heart (soul) to the
Temple is explained typologically: the Temple, representing the Law, is superseded by the human soul, God's
"rationall temple," which through "the lovely shapes of
vertues and graces" *edified* in man accomplishes the perfect "lineaments and proportions" of the Church Militant. For Milton's age resonances such as these were commonly set off by the idea of a temple, and the reference
to temples at the opening of *Paradise Lost* works similarly by calling to mind Solomon's Temple, the Old
Testament archetype of all temples to come, the Temple
which constituted the central human artifact in Christian
theories of art as imitation of God's creation. Such reference underscores and amplifies the poem/cosmos analogy which subtly pervades the first invocation of Milton's
epic: the poet not only invokes here the presiding spirit
of the world's beginning, he also calls on a judge of the
works of men built after the order of this created world.
He seeks guidance from the divine Spirit whose knowledge of both God's creative week and of the temples
which emulate creation makes her ideally suited to assist

in the poet's imitation of the Great Architect's agent, the Son.

This is not all, however. While the word "Temples" in Milton's invocation refers back to "the materiall Temple," man's external creation under the Law, it also, of course, refers simply to the human heart as the prose passage just quoted makes clear. In a sense, then, we can read Milton's lines as a comparison of "th'upright heart and pure" to other hearts not so upright. Yet this in itself again fails to do justice to the richly associative value of the temple as emblem. In the passage from *Church Government* Milton clings tenaciously to the architectural metaphors in his description of the human soul. Similarly in *Paradise Lost* Michael's description of Catholic subversion of the Christian Church (XII, 507–536) conveys the sense of an edified and edifying human soul:

> *What will they [the Roman church] then*
> *But force the Spirit of Grace itself, and bind*
> *His consort Liberty; what, but* unbuild
> His living Temples, built by Faith to stand,
> *Thir own Faith not another's; for on Earth*
> *Who against Faith and Conscience can be heard*
> *Infallible? yet many will presume . . .*
>   *Truth shall retire*
> *Bestuck with sland'rous darts, and* works of Faith
> *Rarely be found . . . .*
>   (XII, 524–537; my emphasis)

This passage, taken in conjunction with the passages already quoted, helps further to demonstrate the expressive richness of Milton's traditional architectural metaphors.

The temple, as an emblem of the heart, serves to fuse "th' upright heart" actively edified after God's "owne prescribed discipline," with the external works that flow from such a heart. Under the Law discipline was external, the Temple, "materiall." Under the Gospel the "works of Faith" are not imposed by external prescription or prohibition; there is no real distance to measure between man's natural impulse rightly known and his true vocation; there is no real boundary between inner life and external action. Man's perfection of his heart and his active endeavors in the world are bound together as "works of Faith." The concept of the heart *as* temple achieves this unity of inner and outer works. In turn this unity helps to explain why the figure of the poet is so central to the argument of *Paradise Lost*.[25]

Early in his career Milton had asserted the unity of outward works and inner discipline by describing the true poet as "a true poem, that is, a composition and pattern of the best and honorablest things."[26] In this antique conception poem and poet merge as they do in *Paradise Lost* when Milton summons at the beginning of his most ambitious poetic flight a spirit that "dost prefer / Before all Temples th' upright heart and pure." Not only can we

[25] On the relation of faith to works see *The Christian Doctrine*, Book II, chapter 1 (C.E., XVII, 1–25). In his treatise Milton makes a logical distinction between inner faith and the works of faith; but it is a distinction which allows no possibility of a separation between faith and works: "we are justified by faith without the works of the law, but not without the works of faith; inasmuch as a living and true faith cannot consist without works . . . ." (C.E., VI, 39). In *Paradise Lost* even such a distinction as this is blurred. The "first fruits" of man's repentance are in fact nothing more external or material than "Sighs / And Prayers" (XI, 22–30).

[26] *The Reason of Church Government*, C.E., III.1, 303.

read these lines as the poet's hope for a heart more fit for his task than other hearts; we can simultaneously read them as a hope for a temple more pleasing to God than lesser temples—for a poem, *Paradise Lost*, as a work of faith built like the first Temple in harmony with God's creation but superior to the archetype as the Gospel is superior to the Law.

VI

One of the most frequently remarked aspects of Milton's epic design has been the studied balancing of positive and negative elements. We have seen that evil in *Paradise Lost*, as if at a loss to discover its true shape, mimics good, and in consequence the shape of evil is often deceptively attractive to unwary humanity. Among other delusive qualities the devils possess a will to action which is uncomfortably close to the poet's own creative energy in that it seeks to imitate divine creativity. Satan's dominion over Hell is a "God-like imitated State" (II, 511); the Serpent tempts Eve with the promise, "ye shall be as Gods" (IX, 708); and Mammon, as we saw in Chapter I, assures his cohorts that Hell can be built after the model of God's making:

> *As he our darkness, cannot we his Light*
> *Imitate when we please? This Desert soil*
> *Wants not her hidden lustre, Gems and Gold;*
> *Nor want we skill or art, from whence to raise*
> *Magnificence . . . .*
>
> (II, 269–273)

Mammon's suggestion here is more than hopeful; Mulciber has already created a grand masterpiece of art in Hell

—Pandaemonium, an ornate structure Milton chooses to compare with the arts of his own world:

> *Let none admire*
> *That riches grow in Hell; that soil may best*
> *Deserve the precious bane. And here let those*
> *Who boast in mortal things, and wond'ring tell*
> *Of* Babel, *and the works of* Memphian *Kings,*
> *Learn how thir greatest Monuments of Fame,*
> *And Strength and Art are easily outdone*
> *By Spirits reprobate . . . .*
>
> (I, 690–697)

If we pause to examine Milton's treatment of infernal creation here, a suggestion already made appears fully confirmed: behind this comparison of hellish and human arts lies an implicit analogy between Pandaemonium and *Paradise Lost.*[27] The infernal structure and the poem resemble each other in their imitations of divine patterns.

The basis for this resemblance is first suggested by the remarkable description of Pandaemonium's construction:

> *A third as soon had form'd within the ground*
> *A various mould, and from the boiling cells*
> *By strange conveyance fill'd each hollow nook:*
> *As in an Organ from one blast of wind*
> *To many a row of Pipes the sound-board breathes.*
> *Anon out of the earth a Fabric huge*
> *Rose like an Exhalation, with the sound*
> *Of Dulcet Symphonies and voices sweet,*
> *Built like a Temple . . . .*
>
> (I, 705–713)

[27] See above, pp. 44–45.

One may suspect in the last line here yet another indirect
allusion to Solomon's Temple, the archetypal human imitation of God's ordered world—a suspicion deepened by
the analogy between music and architectural construction which is the initial feature of the passage. A more
than metaphorical equation of music and measure was
germinal in architectural theories of building as an imitation of the harmonies of God's creation. As Rudolf
Wittkower's excellent study of Renaissance theories of
architecture demonstrates, music was central in humanistic thinking about the arts:

. . . in the closely interrelated encyclopaedia of the arts the
mathematical foundation of music was regarded as exemplary
for the other arts and a familiarity with musical theory became a *sine quo non* of artistic education.[28]

The construction of Pandaemonium, then, imitates or
parodies creation in that it is described by a paradigmatic
analogy between material measure and musical harmony,
the analogy envisioned by medieval and Renaissance
theorists who viewed building as a reflection of the Great
Architect's universal harmonies.

This infernal parody of God's creativity is further suggested by the fact that Satan's rising structure is not just
compared to the sounding of a great organ's pipes; it is
also literally accompanied by music, music which is surely a demonic echo of the song which announces the

[28] Wittkower, p. 103. For a typical seventeenth-century state-
ment of this view by one of Milton's acquaintances see Henry
Wotton, Kt., *The Elements of Architecture* (London, 1624), pp.
246–247. Vitruvius, Wotton relates, as one of "the School of
Pythagoras," "doth determine many things in his profession by
Musical Grounds."

Heavens and Earth rising out of chaos. Moreover, the interior of Satan's infernal structure bears a suggestive resemblance to the work of God's holy week. With "ample spaces" below and "Starry Lamps" above which give light "As from a sky" (I, 725–730), Pandaemonium looks remarkably like the world itself, viewed not from Heaven but, appropriately, from some inferior vantage point.

Other instances of the demonic aping of divine creativity are the "Advent'rous work" (X, 255) of Sin and Death, "a Monument / Of merit high to all th' infernal Host" (X, 258–259), which again parodies the Messiah's building in chaos, and the references to song in Hell. These references in particular are worth examining because in his presentation and comparison of infernal and heavenly song Milton allows himself a strikingly personal response which allows us to see clearly that while he was sensitive to the satanic potential of heavenly imitations, his ultimate concern in displaying parallels between his own and satanic creativity was, as we have seen, to point to crucial differences.

The epic and tragic song of Hell appears most appealingly in Book II:

> *Others more mild*
> *Retreated in a silent valley, sing*
> *With notes Angelical to many a Harp*
> *Thir own Heroic deeds and hapless fall*
> *By doom of Battle; and complain that Fate*
> *Free Virtue should enthrall to Force or Chance.*
> Thir Song was partial, but the harmony
> *(What could it less when Spirits immortal sing?)*

> Suspended Hell, *and took with ravishment*
> *The thronging audience.*
>
> (II, 546–555; my emphasis)

In *Paradise Lost* harmony is the essential quality of the creative act; even here in Hell the decayed remnants of harmonious "notes angelical" are ravishing. But they are *partial*—a key word which is instructively glossed by Sigmund Spaeth:

The fallen angels, similar to the angels in Heaven, instinctively sing in harmony, even though their song is *partial*, i.e., scattered, each one singing for himself alone, without true concent. As usual, Milton is playing on the meaning of the word, using "partial" not only in contrast with "harmony," in the musical sense, but also as suggesting the pride and selfishness of the fallen angels.[29]

While song, then, remains the province of Hell, the devils' fall has produced a fragmented harmony. For Milton, man's sin which "Jarr'd against nature's chime" produced a similar discordancy which only the divinely inspired poet could hope to overcome. The angelic music toward which the poet aspires appears in Book III where Heaven is being described pointedly as the antithesis of Hell:

> . . . *with Preamble sweet*
> *Of charming symphony they introduce*
> *Thir sacred Song, and waken raptures high;*
> *No voice exempt, no voice but well could join*
> *Melodious part, such concord is in Heav'n.*
>
> (III, 367–371)

[29] Sigmund Spaeth, *Milton's Knowledge of Music* (Princeton: Princeton Univ. Press, 1913), p. 114n. See also Patrides' comment on the music of Hell in *Milton and the Christian Tradition*, p. 45.

In contrast to the "partial" song of Hell, the angels' symphonic concord is complete, "no voice exempt." Spaeth's comments again give us a sense of the precision of Milton's musical terminology: the word *symphony* as used by Milton did not, as now, refer chiefly to an orchestra of instruments or voices but to "musical concord, in general."[30] "Such concord is in Heav'n"; Hell can offer only a shattered symphony, a "partial" song. Yet seen in relation to the "hatred, enmity, and strife" of Milton's fallen world even Hell, in its commitment to evil, seems to hold "Firm concord" (II, 495–501).

From such a world the poet's attempt at "harmonious Numbers" is daringly conceived, and its daring is in few places greater than in the inspired transcription of angelic song in Book III. Here, Milton has been accused of a flagrant disregard for the limitations of the narrator's point of view:

> *O unexampled love,*
> *Love nowhere to be found less than Divine!*
> *Hail Son of God, Savior of Men, thy Name*
> *Shall be the copious matter of my Song*
> *Henceforth, and never shall my Harp thy praise*
> *Forget, nor from thy Father's praise disjoin.*
> *Thus they in Heav'n above the starry Sphere,*
> *Thir happy hours in joy and hymning spent.*
>
> (III, 410–417)

The poet, it would seem, shifts his ground from objectivity to an actual participation in the very singing he describes; for a moment at least his voice appears to concord with the heavenly symphony in a dramatically

[30] Spaeth, p. 171.

heightened instance of the lyrical dimension of *Paradise Lost*. The poet has seen the demonic potential of his attempt at a vast symphonic structure and here he longs to separate himself from the devils and their "partial" song. But the attempt remains unsure: while "the copious matter of *my* Song" seems to announce the poet's own intention, this need not be so; the pronoun may also, less appealingly perhaps, refer to each angelic member of the heavenly choir singing for himself, "no voice exempt." The ambiguity is palpable, but to object to it as an example of Milton's alleged imprecision is, I think, to miss the point. While Milton wishes to indicate the direction of his poetic aspiration, he cannot finally force an entrance into the angelic symphony. From a human perspective the Christian poet remains a benighted imitator of divine patterns, blind in a discordant world, in need of heavenly guidance in all its forms. Milton offers himself and his readers a possibility; at last only God can unravel the ambiguity of "my Harp," "my Song."

VII

If, as I have been arguing, Milton conceives of the poet as an ectype of the Son in his roles of prophet and creative agent, we may also suspect that the Son as redeemer played, in some sense, an exemplary role in Milton's poetic self-conception—particularly since *Paradise Lost* seems designed in part to assist the fit reader in the recovery of paradise. Milton, of course, would have been among the first to insist upon the uniqueness of the Son's redemptive office; as fallen poet he makes no claim to crucially intercede for any fallen man. But in his epic

Milton does offer his own energies for the benefit of mankind, and as with Christ this offer has a sacerdotal aspect.

To understand Milton's sense of how a fallen man might ectypically imitate the Son as redeemer, the best place to begin is with Adam and Eve fallen in the garden. Adam, it will be recalled, and subsequently Eve offer to sacrifice themselves in atonement for the crime they jointly share and will bequeath to all mankind (X, 828–841; 933–936). As I have suggested, these selfless impulses in our first parents and their verbal expression seem intended by Milton to recall directly the Son in Heaven offering himself before the assembled angels as mankind's redeemer (III, 236–237).[31] Man's willing offer of atonement is, of course, without ultimate effect in terms of God's justice: only Christ can finally redeem mankind. At the same time, however, our parents self-sacrificial choice, which so clearly echoes the free and selfless offer of the Son's special act, represents, in Milton's mind, the initial stage of regeneration in man. Moreover, as Adam and Eve soon come to realize such regeneration will indeed involve sacrificial "suffering for Truth's sake" (XII, 569) and death. Life in a fallen world will become for them a struggle in which the price of victory will be defeat, and their model for such a life will become their "Redeemer ever blest" (XII, 573).

In Michael's instruction of Adam the exemplary re-

[31] For discussion of these related passages see Hugh MacCallum, " 'Most Perfect Hero': The Role of the Son in Milton's Theodicy," *"Paradise Lost": A Tercentenary Tribute*, B. Rajan, ed. (Toronto: Univ. of Toronto Press, 1969), p. 100; and Joseph Summers, *The Muse's Method* (Cambridge, Mass.: Harvard Univ. Press, 1962), p. 100. Christ repeats his offer to intercede for man at the opening of Book XI (30–44).

deemer appears as a solitary figure, embattled, defeated, yet ultimately victorious in his encounter with the evil Adam's sin has loosed on the world:

> *He shall endure by coming in the Flesh*
> *To a reproachful life and cursed death ....*
> *he shall live hated, be blasphem'd*
> *Seiz'd on by force, judg'd, and to death*
> *condemn'd*
> *A shameful and accurst, nail'd to the Cross*
> *By his own Nation, slain for bringing Life ....*
>
> (XII, 405–414)

This description numbers Christ among a series of solitary heroes who are often taken to be projections of the circumstances of Milton's life in Restoration England. The series begins in Heaven with Abdiel, "faithful found, / Among the faithless, faithful only hee; / Among innumerable false" (V, 896–898). It includes Noah, "In a dark age" "the only Son of light" (XI, 809, 808), and Enoch who amidst "factious opposition" (XI, 644)

> *... spake much of Right and Wrong*
> *Of Justice, of Religion, Truth and Peace,*
> *And Judgment from above: him old and young*
> *Exploded, and had seiz'd with violent hands,*
> *Had not a Cloud descending snatch'd him thence*
> *Unseen amid the throng ....*
>
> (XI, 666–671)

While such stalwarts anticipate Christ's suffering heroism, Milton, a "new" man, can contemplate in retrospect the *perfect* model of solitary fortitude and sacrifice. One need not, of course, turn to Milton's life to find similar-

ities between these heroes and the poet of *Paradise Lost*
who is seen within his poem,

> . . . *fall'n on evil days,*
> *On evil days though fall'n and evil tongues:*
> *In darkness, and with dangers compast round,*
> *And solitude; yet not alone, while thou*
> *Vist'st my slumbers Nightly, or when Morn*
> *Purples the East: still govern thou my Song,*
> *Urania, and fit audience find though few.*
> *But drive far off the barbarous dissonance*
> *Of* Bacchus *and his Revellers, the Race*
> *Of that wild Rout that tore the* Thracian *Bard*
> *In* Rhodope . . . .

> (VII, 25–35)

Here, as we have seen, Milton both compares and contrasts himself to Orpheus (a pagan type of Christ) who,
like Christ and like Enoch, was "seiz'd by violent hands."
This resemblance of Orpheus to Christ and his hebraic
types is, of course, only partial. Unlike Christ and Enoch,
Orpheus, protected only by Calliope, "an empty dream"
(VII, 39), is not "snatch'd . . . thence" by the saving hand
of God. The poet, hoping for better than Calliopean protection from his own nocturnal muse, turns from the example of "the Thracian Bard" toward positive models for
the Christian poet—toward Christ incarnate and those
who like him persevered alone but under God's watchful
eye against the satanic pressures of a fallen world. When
the embattled poet of *Paradise Lost* turns to sing of
Christ in conflict, he again asserts his emulation of his
own ultimate hero by invoking for assistance the same
Spirit,

> ... *who led'st this glorious Eremite*
> *Into the Desert, his Victorious Field*
> *Against the Spiritual Foe ....*
>   (*Paradise Regained*: I, 8–10)

It need not be argued that for Milton, more than for most Christians, the engagement in spiritual conflict was deeply colored by a sense of self-sacrifice. He was, at the writing of *Paradise Lost*, painfully aware of the losses he had suffered not only in pursuit of his own salvation but in his public efforts to create an England of regenerate citizens imbued with the spirit of grace. Milton's forced withdrawal from public life did not, I think, represent an end to his efforts in behalf of the rest of mankind. During the Restoration, in a more profound sense than ever before, his life became a Christian ministry in which the comforts of age were rejected and the arduous labor he had long aimed at was at last taken up. In *Paradise Lost* we are offered this labor, and the poem's texture, as I have been arguing, bears the marks of personal struggle and personal sacrifice. Christlike, Milton engages Satan and, as we have seen, he pursues the battle largely in himself. His open acknowledgment and rejection of the satanic potential of his own lofty aspirations take the shape, as we move through *Paradise Lost*, of mortifications of his own proud nature; and his heroic struggle with the vast problems of decorum posed by his epic subject represent a continuing effort to curb the potential excesses of his own fertile imagination. When in *Paradise Regained* Milton speaks through Christ to reject the allurements of Hellenism, many readers have registered shock; they have felt that here Milton was attack-

ing a part of himself—perhaps the better part. While
such responses make Christ's repudiation of pagan wisdom too absolute, the suggestion that Christ's words represented, for the poet, an agonized self-denial is probably
close to the truth. To depreciate the pagan past was not
easy for Milton; neither was such depreciation a new
development in *Paradise Regained*. *Paradise Lost* anticipates Christ's harsh pronouncement in ways which offer
us, perhaps, a more balanced sense of Milton's sympathies but which, no less than *Paradise Regained*, suggest the painful effort involved in what was finally for
Milton a redirection of his humanist roots. Surely Milton's choice to exercise his talent for the heroic mode
largely in the description of an infernal subject could not
have been easy, and his travesty of epic style in Books V
and VI suggests, as I have argued, an intense reaction to
the appeal homeric flamboyance must have had to a man
of his particular genius. Behind Milton's effort of severe
self-containment lay the example of Christ who appears
in *Paradise Regained* turning from the seductions of
knowledge and power toward his own, unique act of
sacrifice. In imitation of Christ Milton took up the Christian standard and engaged in battle from a position of
weakness and self-denial. Moreover, to repeat, the struggle was for more than John Milton; it was for mankind.
While the shocks of public life had produced in Milton a
restrictive view of his audience, one need not suspect that
Paradise Lost is finally no more than a personal utterance.
As Stanley Fish and others have argued the reading of
Paradise Lost, as much as the writing of it, can be an
exercise in Christian regeneration. Milton, it would seem,
saw it as such, and insofar as his experience as a fallen

man parallels the experiences of his readers, he saw himself, again like Christ, as an exemplar—a "sensible thing" through which others could move toward an apprehension of God's ways.

VIII

Such a self-conception can appear as yet another example of the notorious Miltonic hauteur, but it is again only an aspect of the tension which characterizes the poet's posture in *Paradise Lost*. In displaying himself before his readers Milton couples grandiose aims, grandiose action with humble obedience—a paradoxical posture which finds its ultimate sanction in the example of the Son. It is the Son's willing service to the Father which produces the poem's archetype of opposition to the compelling forces of apostasy and pride. From the paired "consults" of Hell and Heaven wherein Satan and the Son offer themselves in answer to the repeated inquiry, "whom shall we send" (II, 403; compare to III, 213ff.) to the contrast between the "universal hiss" (X, 508) and the "Halleluiahs" (VII, 634) which greet in turn the Devil and the Messiah as they return from their respective missions of destruction and creation, Milton overtly and schematically opposes the Son to Satan. But from the first the imitation of the Son's example has been a precarious aspiration for the poet, an aspiration fraught with the dangers of satanic overreaching. In his initial invocation the poet magniloquently seeks to imitate the Son's creative agency. The Heavens and Earth *rise* out of chaos and the ascending movement which describes this first expression of God's creative love for man echoes throughout Milton's opening lines to characterize the poet's own attempt to rise to the height of his great argument, "to soar / Above th' Aonian Mount" (I, 14–15), and to place himself boldly in the prophetic line of which Christ was the exemplar. The counterweight to the audacity of these aspirations accompanies them in yet another oblique allusion to the Son—an allusion which finally marks the difference between ectype and model. Milton seeks the heavenly power present at "Siloa's Brook" (I, 11) and thereby recalls a scriptural episode of obvious and poignant significance to himself:

And his disciples asked him, saying, Master, who did sin, this man or his parents, that he was born blind? Jesus answered, Neither hath this man sinned, nor his parents: but that the works of God should be made manifest in him.
                                        (John, 9:2–3)

Thus on one hand Milton, in attempting to illuminate God's ways for men, strove adventurously to imitate the agency of the Son who, manifesting God's goodness, "by creation first brought / Light out of darkness" (XII, 472–473); but at the same time "Light out of darkness" as administered to the blind man by Christ, "the light of the world" (John, 9:5), epitomized for Milton his utter dependence on God: "So much the rather thou Celestial Light / Shine inward" (III, 51–52).

Afterword

Paradise Regained
and the Miltonic Hero

HAVING COME this far in pursuit of Milton's epic exemplars, I would like to comment briefly on the Christ of *Paradise Regained*. What we have learned of the Christian hero in *Paradise Lost* is surely useful in any approach to Milton's song of "Recover'd Paradise"; and in turn this second heroic poem can help us, I think, to focus one of the central issues we have been pursuing here: Milton's relation to his own poetic structures.

The question of genre has occupied a prominent place in critical commentary on *Paradise Regained*, but the question of subject, which has seemed somewhat less pressing, is also of considerable interest. Briefly stated, it is worth inquiring why Milton chose this preliminary skirmish between Christ and Satan to describe the recovery of paradise. *Paradise Lost* looks forward to the Son's heroic recovery of what Adam has forfeited by sin:

> *. . . this God-like act*
> *Annuls thy doom, the death thou shouldst have*
> *di'd,*

In sin for ever lost from life ....
                                        (XII, 427–429)

Yet *Paradise Regained*, a poem clearly responsive to the promise of redemption, does not deal directly with the Passion ("this God-like act") but turns instead to Christ's temptations in the desert, wherein his victory seems more immediately personal than universal, more manlike than Godlike—hardly a victory to redeem all mankind. Of course one can read this episode in Christ's life as an anticipation of the Savior's ultimate triumph, and it is clear that Milton intended it to be read in this way. But why such indirection? Milton had already attempted one poem on the Passion, and while in his youth he soon retreated from the subject, surely he could not now offer the excuse of insufficient years.

If we turn to the generic tradition behind *Paradise Regained*, Milton's choice of subject appears, if anything, less obvious. Barbara Kiefer Lewalski's valuable study of this tradition cites only one example of a brief epic centering on Christ's temptations in the wilderness,[1] and while Mrs. Lewalski suggests several plausible reasons for Milton's having chosen this episode as his subject,[2]

[1] *Milton's Brief Epic* (Providence: Brown Univ. Press, 1966), p. 66.

[2] See in particular ch. 5. Here, Mrs. Lewalski argues, among other things, that (1) the events of the book of Job, which was in Milton's mind a prime instance of brief epic, readily suggested the action of Christ's temptation (Job's suffering, however, had also suggested Christ's Passion to others); (2) that this episode in Christ's life "could be treated as a transmutation of the single combat of hero and antagonist, the event which is traditionally the epitome and climax of an epic" (p. 104); and (3) that it lent itself to the discussion of Christ's role as head of his church (pp.

her review of the history of biblical epic does not, I think, finally make clear why the Passion would not have been at least as obvious a choice. John Steadman, in his carefully developed study of Christ as Milton's model for Christian heroism, seems openly puzzled by Milton's avoidance (with, of course, the one abortive exception) of a poem dealing with Christ's supreme heroic act:

In Messiah's ministry of redemption Milton found the norm of Christian heroism for both of his epics, but not (paradoxically) an epic subject. Except for the incomplete lines on "The Passion," he never, apparently, devoted a poem to what would seem to be the logical material for a Christian heroic poet—the crucifixion and resurrection. Though both of his epics represent these "godlike acts" as the supremely heroic enterprise, the actual arguments of both poems concern events preliminary to this "glorious work" . . . . Milton never assayed a *Christiad*, the logical objective for a Christian poet.[3]

Steadman's response to the problem he raises is admittedly tentative: he suspects Milton wished to avoid following the notable precedent of Vida, and, more assertively, he supposes the Gospel accounts of the Passion offered Milton "little scope to invent."[4] Steadman also notices, as others have noticed, the anticipatory aspect of *Paradise Regained*, but the fact remains that Milton's title is not *Paradise About to be Regained*. It is not un-

106–107). Most tellingly, I think, she also suggests that Milton rejected the Passion as a subject because it would "virtually demand ritualistic rather than dramatic treatment" (p. 109; see Steadman's observations below).

[3] John M. Steadman, *Milton's Epic Characters* (Chapel Hill: The Univ. of North Carolina Press, 1959), p. 69.

[4] Steadman, p. 70.

reasonable to assume that despite the epic's clear anticipation of the act which redeems all men, Milton saw here, in Christ's debate with Satan, an actual recovery of paradise—as he says, "Eden rais'd in the waste Wilderness" (*Paradise Regained*, I, 7).

If the question of Milton's subject is stated differently, his motives for choosing to write of Christ's temptations become more accessible. In what sense, we may ask, does Christ here raise Eden in the wilderness? *Paradise Lost*, it will be recalled, offers a double sense in which paradise may be regained. The ultimate recovery will occur at the end of time: "then the Earth / Shall be Paradise, far happier place / Than this of Eden, and far happier days" (XII, 463–465); but prior to this world's dissolution mankind is offered a paradise within, a paradise which like man's final place of rest results from Christ's redemptive sacrifice. The Passion was, for Milton, a unique act of eschatological consequence. While the first regenerative stirrings of Adam and Eve can echo the Son's offer of atonement, man finally cannot redeem man.[5] Yet in the second sense of Eden's recovery man clearly participates, and because of this, I think, Milton chose Christ's temptations as the subject of *Paradise Regained*. In *Paradise Lost*, as we saw in the preceding chapter, the Son is presented as the ultimate exemplar for humanity. In *Paradise Regained* his role is clearly the same; but here Milton is more centrally concerned to delineate Christ's exemplary aspect. In Christ's resistance to Satan, Milton saw a crucial instance of the labor all men must undertake; such labor was, in fact, essential to Milton's understanding of the individual's recovery of an inward paradise.

[5] See above, pp. 175–176.

What Christ's temptations in *Paradise Regained* represent, then, is an action for all men to imitate; they represent the *process* of recovery, the recovery of a paradise within.[6]

Milton presents Christ in the wilderness contemplating the rudiments of his own life. Through his holy meditations and his confrontation with the tempter, Christ comes to comprehend the spirit of God within him; he discovers what it means to be the "Son of God"—a discovery which is special to him but which also, as Satan himself realizes, bears a crucial, though lower, significance for man and angel alike. What man must realize to recover paradise is the unceasing attendance of God's spirit; as Adam puts it, man must learn "to walk / As in his presence" (XII, 562–563). Such wayfaring is what Christ constantly affirms in *Paradise Regained* as he considers where he has been and where he must go. Thus exemplified by Christ, the Miltonic hero is the man who confronts his own experience and with the conviction of God's spirit within him considers his own direction:

> *Musing and much revolving in his breast*
> *How best the mighty work he might begin . . .*
> *He enter'd now the bordering Desert wild,*
> *And with dark shades and rocks environ'd round,*
> *His holy Meditations thus pursu'd.*
>
> *O what a multitude of thoughts at once*
> *Awak'n'd in me swarm, while I consider*
> *What from within I feel myself, and hear*

[6] That this may have been Milton's intention has not escaped critical notice. William R. Parker makes the point with admirable brevity in *Milton: A Biography* (Oxford: The Clarendon Press, 1968), I, 616.

What from without comes often to my ears,
Ill sorting with my present state compar'd.
When I was yet a child, no childish play
To me was pleasing, all my mind was set
Serious to learn and know, and thence to do . . .
The Law of God I read, and found it sweet . . .
                    at our great Feast
I went into the Temple, there to hear
The Teachers of our Law, and to propose
What might improve my knowledge or their own:
And was admir'd by all: yet this not all
To which my Spirit aspir'd; victorious deeds
Flam'd in my heart, heroic acts . . . .
                    (*Paradise Regained*, I, 196–212)

In contemplation of his own acts and potential for action, the Miltonic hero discovers God in himself. Through temptation he is perfected in obedience and rectitude. So it is with Milton's Samson, confronting in Gaza the iniquities of his own life, and finding at last the "strong motions" of God's spirit directing him to heroic action. So also with Milton himself who, as I have argued, pursues in *Paradise Lost* a Christian adventure in which he responds, like Christ, to "What from within" he feels and "What from without comes often to . . . [his] ears." In his epic he confronts the dangers of pride and apostacy latent in his learning, his revolutionary past, and his present aspirations; in contemplation of his own experience he struggles, as best he can, to deliver his powers into the guiding hands of God.

Louis Martz, in his provocative essay on *Paradise Regained*, develops at length the sense of Christ's self-discovery that I am emphasizing here. My debt to his reading is obvious and extensive. In viewing *Paradise Regained* as a meditative poem, he finds the voice of Milton speaking throughout:

> . . . in this inward speaking of the meditative mind, all "characters," all speeches, are enveloped within, and suffused with, the controlling voice of the meditator himself. That mind is exploring its own problems, as well as those of mankind, through the speeches of the "characters," who have indeed no separate existence, whose very function is to take upon themselves the meditative voice of the narrator.[7]

In this view *Paradise Regained* becomes a radical instance of what I have been suggesting with respect to *Paradise Lost*—an instance of a poem in which the concerns of the narrator are repeatedly felt in and through the words and actions of his protagonists. Yet while Martz is surely correct in feeling the pervasive influence of Milton's voice in the "characters" of *Paradise Regained*, it is also fair to say that in this poem the action centers on a single projection of the poet's consciousness—Christ, the perfect hero—whereas in *Paradise Lost* such a center is lacking. While *Paradise Regained* offers a Christ speaking inclusively for Milton, in *Paradise Lost* the poet, lacking a central spokesman, must obtrude himself more directly. If we look in *Paradise Lost* for a clear and extended example of the Miltonic hero, of the man who persistently labors to discover God in himself, we do not find it, I think, in Adam, who falters and is left at the brink of his journey toward regeneration, or in the Son whose crucial role is removed from the poem's human center. Rather we find it in the poet. From the outset Milton presents his aspira-

[7] *The Paradise Within*, p. 191.

tions to the knowledge of God as a continuously precarious effort to respond to the heavenly motions within him; in contemplating his own struggle he contemplates the history of mankind's fall and redemption; he realizes the workings of providence in his poem and in himself; he is (so he hopes) his own Christian hero.

We have, in effect, returned to Saurat's contention that "The hero of *Paradise Lost* was Milton himself," but in a new sense. As Martz has said, Milton's presence in *Paradise Lost* is "no mere self-indulgence."[8] Milton does not unwittingly allow the force of his own personality to distort what was intended as an objective rendering of the fall of man. Objectivity was hardly the issue. Rather, as we have seen, by offering himself as an example of the Christian in conflict, Milton was concerned to turn the meaning of his own encounter with God's ways toward all mankind, to become himself an heroic pattern.

[8] *The Paradise Within*, p. 106.

Index

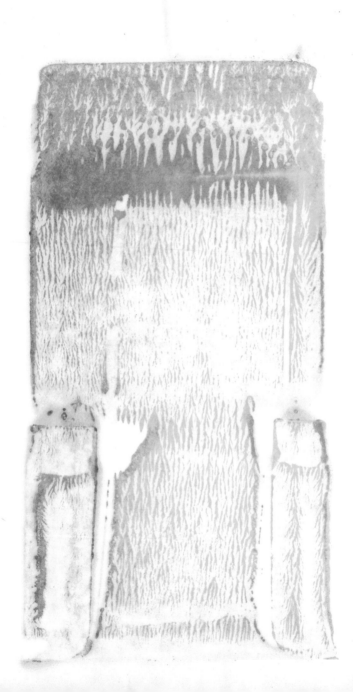